Wisdom

FROM THE

Women

WE LOVE

LIFE LESSONS FILLED
WITH WOMEN'S WISDOM

COMPILED BY
Elza Spaedy

EDITED BY
Jennifer Crelen

Table of Contents

From Our Beloved Pastor

It is said that God works in mysterious ways. That has certainly been the case with this particular work. Elza has been attentive to the promptings of the Spirit from the beginning and has been tremendously attentive to the ways in which He has guided the project. The world in which we live often overlooks and undervalues the important witness of women of faith. Yet, these pages illustrate that there are many women today who are following in the footsteps of some of the most inspiring women of the Sacred Scriptures, such as Ruth, Esther, Elizabeth, Mary Magdalen, and of course, Our Blessed Mother.

The wisdom that you will encounter here beautifully relates God's power to work in the midst of life difficulties when we willingly turn to Him and allow Him to show us the way. I pray that all who read these pages might be richly blessed by the stories of these strong, faithful women and that their efforts here might encourage you to share your stories along the way.

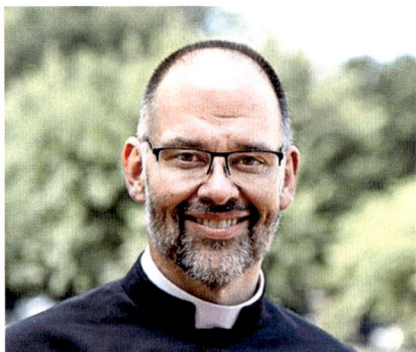

In Christ,

Father John Putnam, Pastor
St. Mark Catholic Church
Huntersville, NC

Dedication

I dedicate this book to our beautiful, most pure and the ONLY perfect role model we have as women: Our Blessed Mother. Mary Queen of all Wisdom, pray for us and teach us to be saints!

To my very selfless mom who taught me so much of what I know. To my loving and very supportive husband David and our three wonderful and kind children Bella, Bree and Tristan. You guys are my most precious gifts from God and words can't describe just how much I love you.

My soul proclaims
the greatness of the Lord;
my spirit rejoices in
God my savior.
For He has looked upon
his handmaid's lowliness;
behold, from now on all ages
will call me blessed.
The Mighty One has done
great things for me
and holy is His name.

Luke 1:46-49

Introduction

The idea for this book came to me one sleepless night not too long ago after a visit from the Holy Spirit. In a matter of about one hour, God filled my soul with the vision for this beautiful book you are holding in your hands right now. I can't even begin to describe the excitement I felt contacting my close friends about this idea. Their overwhelmingly positive and supportive response reassured me that this is indeed God's will. As with all my inspirations lately, I let God lead me to the right people to make creating this book possible.

My prayer is that after you read it, you'll be encouraged to remember and even write down the wisdom given to you from the extraordinary women in your lives. This project is also an answer to a prayer... That my own daughters Bella and Bree will encounter amazing and strong women of faith that can help them continue to grow into beautiful godly women. The pages of this book are filled with personal stories from women of all different ages and backgrounds. Hopefully, their shared wisdom will help you navigate this crazy world we live in and keep your eyes on the prize of Heaven. I love reading about the lives of the saints and find them very inspiring, but I also believe that modern women are eager to hear from other Christian women who are living in today's world and facing the difficult challenges of our time.

We added a few discussion questions at the end of each chapter in hopes that you may want to use this book in small group studies, or maybe with your own "coffee group" every week. I know that my friends and I would have loved a book like this when we got together for those memorable weekly gatherings in Bismarck.

May God bless you and your families abundantly! With much love, Elza.

A Call Within a Call

An apostolate is a Lay Christian organization "directed to serving and evangelizing the world," most often associated with the Catholic Church. About three years ago I felt called by God to start a beautiful women's apostolate beginning with a Mother-Daughter Spiritual Brunch. Our mission statement is simple: "To inspire mothers, daughters, and women in general through the guidance of the Holy Spirit with inspirational talks and practical ways to live our beautiful Catholic faith in our everyday lives." With the help of a small but very dedicated group of women, we will be celebrating our 3rd Mother-Daughter Spiritual Brunch this May.

When I was inspired to put this event together, I also felt the Lord was telling me this is only the beginning. Now it's becoming clear to me that this book is indeed "a call within a call." I am borrowing that phrase from one of my favorite saints, Saint Mother Teresa. In 1946 on the way to an annual retreat, Mother Teresa was asked by God to begin a new religious community. That community would become The Missionaries of Charity, dedicated to serving the poorest of the poor throughout the world. While I have not been called to start my own religious community, I am listening to the Spirit. God wants me to gather and share the wisdom from women of all ages and backgrounds to begin essential discussions about living our faith. I believe this is an extension of God's vision for the women's apostolate and the spiritual brunch. This is proof that if we find time to listen to Him, He will do amazing things in us and through us! If you would like to know more about the women's apostolate and the Mother-Daughter Spiritual Brunch, please visit our website at mdspiritualbrunch.org or contact us at mdspiritualbrunch@gmail.com. We would love to help you get a Mother-Daughter Spiritual Brunch started in your own parish. Together and guided by the Holy Spirit we can continue His kingdom here on earth!

Foreword

One cannot sit with Elza without picking up on her zeal for the Lord. In our first conversations, we could feel the loving presence of the Holy Spirit in the room as Elza shared what the Lord has done for her. When Elza asked me to contribute a story for this book, I paused for a second, in awe of what our Lord was about to do *through* her. I thought about all the times that I have sat with women over the years and felt blessed by hearing their stories. I remembered how in every woman's story, I could see a part of myself. I remembered wishing on so many occasions that these women could hear the things I've heard and know for certain that they are not alone in their struggles. I'm reminded of a quote from *A Return to Love* by Marianne Williamson, "We were born to make manifest the glory of God that is within us. It is not just in some of us; it is in everyone. And as we let our own light shine, we unconsciously give other people permission to do the same. As we are liberated from our own fear, our presence automatically liberates others."

The women who have contributed to this book have consented to bearing their souls and sharing how the Lord has worked in their lives. They have followed the promptings of the Spirit to share the message that the Lord has placed on their heart. "Be strong and courageous, do not be afraid or tremble at them, for the LORD your God is the one who goes with you. He will not fail you or forsake you." Deuteronomy 31:6 (NASB)

God is present in our stories. He tells us through Scripture that He will never leave us. We also know that God works everything for good for those who love Him. Therefore, when we share our stories, we are witnessing to God's work and Love in our lives. We encounter God through presence and vulnerability. My hope for all who read this book is that you will feel uplifted by the stories of these women and be empowered to share your own.

Let your light shine.

Your Sister in Christ,

Christine Wisdom

You are *beautiful* in every way,

my love, there is *no flaw* in you!

SONG OF SONGS 4:7

~Beauty Is Only Skin Deep~

Written by: Elza Spaedy

Brazil is known for its beautiful women. Famous supermodels like Gisele Bundchen, Adriana Lima and Alessandra Ambrosio were all born there. I too was born and raised in Brazil and in my personal experience the emphasis on outer beauty borders on obsessive.

Not that it's much different here in the United States as I'm sure you already know. This unrealistic ideal puts a tremendous amount of pressure on women to look perfect or feel "less than." It's very common to hear of women going under the knife after having babies by getting breast implants and tummy tucks. This brings me to my first story, back when I was about 12 or 13 and becoming a young lady. I'll never forget one day I decided to ask my very humble and selfless mom if she would ever consider having one of these procedures. Keep in mind, my mom had 11 babies in less than 15 years! Looking back I think of how laughable that question must have been to a selfless woman like her. My mom simply looked at me, smiled and said, "Oh honey, no I wouldn't do that. What kind of message would I be sending you and your sisters? Someday you'll understand."

That "someday" came 23 years later when I was married to my husband David and living in South Florida, a place also known for its beautiful women. I was in my mid-thirties, and I had just given birth to our second daughter, my sweet Bree. Some of my friends and neighbors were getting plastic surgery, changing things on their body they considered to be "wrong." Because my faith wasn't as strong as it is today, I considered having a procedure or two myself. One night I confided in David that after we were done having kids, I would like to invest in a few physical "enhancements." I was falling into the world's trap of thinking there was something wrong with my post-baby body. David was adamantly against the idea and told me he loves me just the way I am. I felt somewhat relieved hearing that from him, but I secretly thought if I still want this in a few years I'm sure I can find a way to convince him. Thanks to the Holy Spirit, my mom's words of wisdom came back to me, and I suddenly realized what she meant all those years ago. I was the mother of two precious baby girls who would grow up to be women looking to me to be their first role model. This world may want us to believe that our moms are not supposed to be our ideal role models, but my mom is and always will be a role model to me.

Fast forward 12 years to today and my girls are now teenagers, the same age I was when I asked my mom that naive question. I thank God that I had my mom's words of wisdom come flashing back to me during that confusing time when I was bombarded with so many lies in the world. I want my daughters and all women to know that there's absolutely nothing wrong with our post-baby bodies. Our sons also need to grow up knowing that women are so much more than body parts and to never put any pressure on the women they love to make those changes to their bodies. Imagine our beautiful Blessed Mother feeling the pressure to have one of those procedures done after giving birth to Jesus? That's absolutely ridiculous, right! She knew God had chosen her to be the vessel to bring salvation into the world and I'm sure she didn't think any less of her body afterward.

On the contrary, I'm sure she was in awe of the entire experience and couldn't stop thanking God for it! Cardinal Joseph Mindszenty said it best. "Mothers are closer to God the creator than all other creatures. God joins forces with mothers in performing his act of creation. What on God's good earth is more glorious than this: to be a mother?"

Let us not be fooled by these worldly lies that try so hard to demean the mother's position of being chosen by God. If we are truly striving to live holy lives that reflect the teachings of the gospel, then we as women must start by being honest with ourselves and helping each other by sharing our stories.

The inspiration for this book is not coming from me but from the Holy Spirit himself. John 16:13 says "When the Spirit of Truth comes, he will guide you into all the truth, for he will not speak in his own authority, but whatever he hears he will speak, and he will declare to you the things that are to come."

Questions to Consider

1. Are you or someone you know contemplating changing their physical appearance because of the societal pressures placed on women? How can our inward beauty and virtue be radiated on the outside?

2. How can we all encourage each other to focus on the salvation of our souls and not on the passing things of this world?

BUT SEEK FIRST THE *kingdom of God* AND HIS *righteousness,* AND ALL THESE THINGS WILL BE GIVEN TO YOU BESIDES.

- MATTHEW 6:33 -

~ He Comes First ~

Written by: Jennifer Creter

The big television career... that's what I wanted, and I was going to get it no matter what. People I loved are going to get hurt? That's the price I was willing to pay to fulfill MY dream. It was all about me then, an incredibly selfish young career woman on the rise. At least that's what I thought before God put the breaks on this train barreling down the wrong track.

"News nuns," it's a term used to describe unmarried women who work in television news and devote all their time and energy to the job. I was one phone call away from choosing that path. Thinking back to that time I can hardly believe how screwed up my priorities were. How did they get that way? I know exactly how it happened because I was putting my selfish desires before God.

I discovered a passion for television news when I was in college. I worked for our campus TV station, and it was there that my love for breaking news blossomed. It was exhilarating for me to update scripts at the last minute, or to run out with a photographer to cover a breaking news story. We used to say, "If it bleeds, it leads." Stories that break my heart today didn't faze me in the least back then.

Right after graduation, I was hired as a producer in my hometown of Dayton, Ohio. I was a good writer, and I was promoted quickly. I was the low woman on the totem pole and would work the shifts no one else wanted. That meant I was absent for many family celebrations, and if I did manage to show up I was usually exhausted. "It's ok," I said to myself, "My career needs to be my number one priority right now."

I got engaged to my college sweetheart when we were 22. When my career took off, I felt like he was slowing me down. He had a good job and wanted to get married and raise a family in Ohio. So, I did what I thought was best for me, and called off our wedding the same day I was supposed to mail out the invitations. I left him back in Dayton with a broken heart while I pursued the next promotion. I've never regretted my decision to wait to get married; clearly, I wasn't ready! I do however wish I had handled it differently.

After about a year of working in Dayton, I was offered a producing job an hour away in Columbus, Ohio. I was only there for about a year when Cleveland called. Each move up provided more money, more power, and more responsibility. During these years I rarely saw my tight-knit Catholic family. But we have to make sacrifices to make it to the big time, right?

At age 26, I was promoted to the job of Executive Producer of the 5 and 6 o'clock news at WJW-TV in Cleveland. I was responsible for overseeing two hours of live broadcast, five days a week. I had about 30 people reporting to me, as you can imagine I lived and breathed the news. I rarely went to church or made time to pray. I was spiritually empty and filling my mind with all the wrong things.

One busy afternoon I got a phone call from a TV station in New York City. "We have a job opening for a producer, and we'd like to fly you here for an interview." It was the call I had been waiting for, but something stopped me from giving them an immediate yes. I needed time to think about it, so I told them I'd call them back the next morning.

That night, the Holy Spirit paid me a visit. What does that feel like? It's hard to explain, but it's an overwhelming sense of knowing what to do. Sometimes it's not the answer you were expecting or maybe even want to hear. Not only did He tell me to turn down the job in New York, but also to leave the news business altogether! I was stunned at what the Holy Spirit was urging me to do. With the help of God's grace, I took a good hard look at my life and where it was heading. The news business was becoming a toxic environment for me, turning me into a person I no longer knew. God was leading me out of that life, and finally, I was listening!

My true vocation became clear that night. I was to focus on my family and to work on building one of my own. I didn't know who I was going to marry or when, but I knew my current life wasn't my ultimate calling. I'm not suggesting mothers shouldn't work outside the home, but if your job is consuming your life- it's time to review your priorities. My loving mom selflessly stayed home to focus on us, her five kids. Many sacrifices were made by both of my parents to raise a large family on one income. Somehow they found a way to pay for all five of us to have 12 years of Catholic education. My mom and dad have been married for 56 years. They'll tell you they always put God first, their marriage second, and the kids third. I learned that while careers are important, they should never come before your relationship with God or your family. Try to focus on *who* you are, not just *what* you are. My words of wisdom to the younger generation are to make sure your priorities in order, and if they are God will show you the way to eternal happiness.

As always, God reveals His plan for our lives in His time. You see, there was a purpose for that job in Cleveland. That's where I met two of my closest girlfriends at the TV station, and my best friend of all – my husband, Tom. We were only coworkers during my time there, but right before I moved back to Dayton, he invited me to a Cleveland Indians baseball game. He introduced me to his entire family, and that's when I knew he was someone special. He comes from a big Catholic family too, and we compliment each other nicely. God has blessed us with two loving boys to raise. Aidan and Will are teenagers now, both in high school and growing in their Catholic faith. Tom and I will celebrate our 19th wedding anniversary this summer, and while every marriage goes through challenges – we are committed to making ours last. Attending mass together weekly and actively volunteering and participating in our parish community help keep our family unit strong. Remember your priorities ladies: God, spouse, children, and then everything else.

Questions to Consider

1. It's not always easy putting God first when making important decisions in our lives. Do you feel like your priorities are in order? How can we as Christian women help each other think about choosing God's will before our own selfish desires?

2. Many mothers believe their children's needs should come before their spouse's. How can this order of priorities hurt the family unit in the long run?

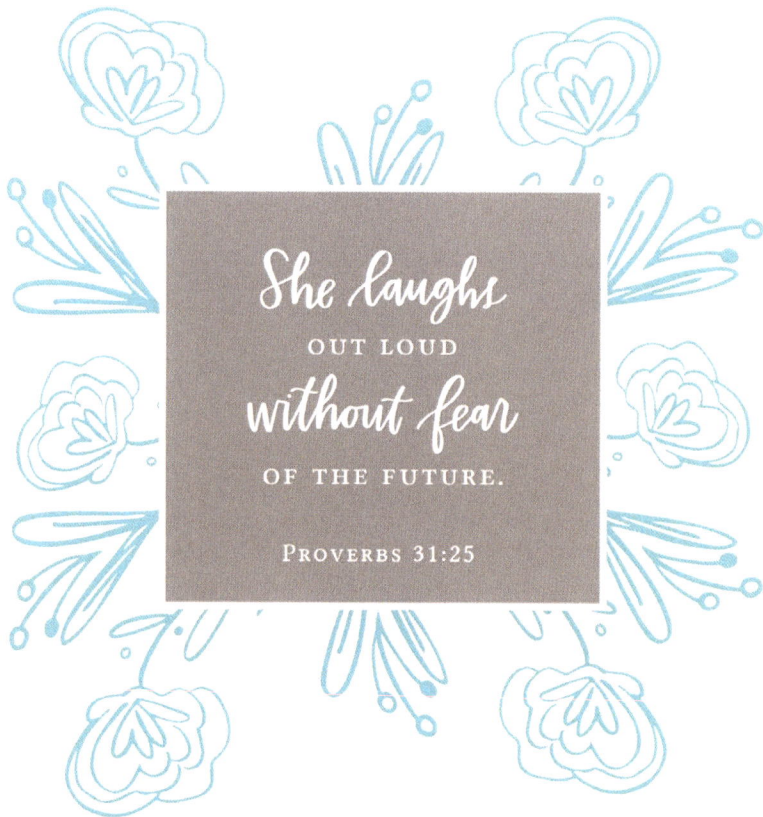

She laughs

OUT LOUD

without fear

OF THE FUTURE.

PROVERBS 31:25

~ Two Marys Guide Me From Heaven ~

Written By: Jean Whelan

My mother's laugh was contagious and lighthearted. It moved my soul to know all is well as I listened to her from across the room. Seared into my memory as a reminder of what an authentic Catholic woman sounds like, my mother's laugh would become my guide.

"She laughs without fear of the future" was the perfect description of my mother that I recalled as I listened to a family friend read from Proverbs 31 during my mother's funeral Mass. Twenty-six years old and pregnant with my first born, I was too young to have my mother leave this earth and go to Heaven.

Mary Kay Ferris' untimely death at the age of 52 rocked our community. As a healthy young mother of six children, she was misdiagnosed with a fatal blood clot. My family, the Saint Michael Church community, and the town of Cary, North Carolina were devastated. Over 1,000 people attended her funeral Mass to comfort my family and to say goodbye to a woman who loved the Lord deeply. Most of the people would comment on her great love and her reassuring laugh. They loved her and when in her presence, wanted to soak in the joy she exuberated.

As I was sitting on the edge of my mother's bed the evening of her funeral Mass, her glasses on the nightstand grabbed my attention. My mother wore those glasses for as long as I could remember. The words, "You take nothing with you to Heaven," were radiating in my heart and in my head as if my mother was speaking to me. The new way of communicating with my mother had begun. I recalled the words of wisdom spoken to me from one of my mother's friends, an 87-year-old woman by the name of Henriette. "There is a thin veil between Heaven and Earth."

With immediate strength, I vowed to give up my earthly goals of fortune and career success to seek the Lord with all my heart, my mind, and my will. My mother was in Heaven, and I wanted to be with her when my time on Earth was finished. God heard my promise in my heart, and He answered.

A few months after the death of my mother, my sweet Mary Kathryn was born. Jerry and I had just moved to Pennsylvania, and my father had made the trip north to visit us. Sitting at the kitchen table, my father passed me a book. "Jeannie, I think you should read this book," he said, sliding across the table a small bright orange book by Louis de Montfort titled, *Consecration to Jesus through Mary*. I picked up the book and turned it over to the back cover. The phrase, "The quickest, surest way to Jesus" piqued my interest. Wow, the Lord was already fulfilling my promise of seeking Him with all my heart and all my soul. My father continued by explaining that he had completed the consecration to Our Lady and he recommended I do the same. I read the book, and even though I had difficulty with the wording and some of the concepts, I decided to consecrate myself to the Blessed Mother. I needed the Queen of Heaven to be a mother to me with my earthly mother in Heaven working at her side.

The Blessed Mother took hold of my hand and - later as I grew to know her more intimately - my heart. She began educating me in my lack of knowledge about the Catholic Church. I was introduced to the Holy Spirit through Mother Angelica on EWTN. Taking notes during many of her TV shows, I soon learned about the gifts of the Holy Spirit. I didn't know at the time we had received gifts at our Confirmation. Soon I was attending retreats, teaching religious education, studying scripture, and going to daily Mass. As the years passed, Mary took charge of the ministries I would lead, create, and organize. Through prayer, she guided my family on where to live, who we should hang out with, and she even picked our dog, Charlie! Mary developed and helped me become aware of the talents God has given me, and also the talents of my children. She is my guide in all things. On a fun note, She is the best interior decorator! Mary just recently helped me plan the most beautiful wedding for my daughter Mary Kathryn and her husband, Joe. Mary hand-picked Joe too.

Both heavenly mothers Mary Kay Ferris and Our Blessed Mother have passed their peace and joy onto me. My mom lost her mother at the age of 26 as well, while pregnant with her baby girl, me. Her mother Helen was misdiagnosed with breast cancer, and she also had a deep love for the Blessed Mother. Helen was written about in the newspaper for the construction of a grotto to Our Lady that she built in her backyard. My family history runs deep with women who love Mary and only had a few short years to form their daughters. My mother's laugh is my guidepost. I am now 54 and have the joy of looking back and seeing God's blessed assurance throughout my life. My mom could laugh without fear of the future because, like me, she had her mother Helen and the Blessed Mother guiding her from Heaven.

Questions to Consider

1. Are you familiar with the *Consecration to Mary Through Jesus*? If not, are you interested in knowing more about it? If so, take a look at **33daystomorningglory.com** by Father Michael Gaitley.

2. Have you traced back your own devotion to Mary to other women in your family? Your mom, grandmother or an aunt maybe? Do you think you'll be passing down that devotion to your own children?

WHOEVER DRINKS THE WATER

I SHALL GIVE WILL *never thirst;*

THE WATER I SHALL GIVE WILL BECOME

IN HIM A SPRING OF WATER

WELLING UP TO *eternal life.*

JOHN 4:14

~ My Path to Surrender ~

Written by: Erin Zamora

As the youngest of four children, I grew up in what I considered to be a typical Catholic family in Northeast Ohio. By all accounts our life was normal: we went to good schools, attended Mass every Sunday, and wanted for very little. On the surface, I was blessed, at least materially. At the age of 12 however, my entire world fell apart when my parents announced they were getting a divorce.

Our family was one of the first families in our Catholic community to go through this separation, at a time when divorce was nowhere near as common as it is today. The effects it had on my brothers and myself as children, teenagers, and into our adult lives still continues today.

The immediate trauma that comes from divorce has been explained as if a parent were to walk into a child's room, break every toy that the child holds dear to their heart, and leave them to try to put the pieces back together, alone. The announcement of my parent's divorce completely shattered our worlds. I'll never forget the day they sat me down with one of my brothers after school. I remember thinking, "Where are my other brothers – what is going on?" My parents told us that they were getting a divorce, my father was moving out, and that two of my brothers would be leaving with him. That's when my brother started to cry, and no one even tried to comfort him. I remember sitting there, thinking, "How could this be happening: I never even saw my parents fight; what does this mean for our family?" While my brother cried, I stayed silent. We were both heartbroken and confused. In a nutshell: we were left to put the pieces of our young lives back together, alone. My family has never been the same since.

Soon after my father left, a new, much younger girlfriend moved in with him and my two brothers. She was near the age of my oldest brother.

Besides being embarrassed, I felt terrible for my mother – a feeling that I struggled with considerably over the years; one that she never shielded me from. I think it brought her some comfort to know that I was on "her side." Around the same time my father began to do very well with his business and to try to smooth things over after the divorce, he showered us with gifts, vacations, and an all-around attitude that money can fix any problem. I was left feeling conflicted and confused.

My parents, while very similar in some ways, differed significantly in others. They were so young, just teenagers when they got married and started having kids. My mother's parenting style was strict and rigid, rarely showing us any affection. But she was there, present in our day to day lives. My father was more relaxed with rules and discipline, but I couldn't count on him. He was living his new life with his second wife. The divorce highlighted the selfish aspects of my parents' personalities. Their lack of introspection left us to deal with the flood of negative feelings that come from essentially being emotionally abandoned.

Each one of us coped with our feelings in different ways. My two oldest brothers chose a life of self-destruction, fueled with years of alcohol and drug abuse, violence, and poor decision making. This downward spiral with drugs led to my brother Matt's tragic death at the young age of 22. My other brother and I did our best to stay out of trouble. We tried to make good decisions in school and in life, but we had very little support emotionally or spiritually from either of our parents. Matt's death left our family even more fragmented. We all struggled. We grew further apart and once again, we were left to figure it out on our own.

By the grace of God and my brother looking down from Heaven, I fell in love with Matt's best friend Daniel, and we married young. My husband knew my brother very well – they were, as he endearingly says, "thick as thieves." Daniel was the one friend who was always there for Matt. When my brother passed away, I found a powerful connection with Daniel, one that couldn't be replicated with any other person.

I am thankful for this blessing every day of my life. Matt would have wanted me to be taken care of, the way that he would look out for me – by any means necessary – and my husband has done just that. In my relationship with Daniel I found a piece of my brother, and through our marriage, I discovered what it means to love, and be loved, unconditionally. In Matt's death, new life was born with the creation of our family.

My husband and I had four kids in quick succession. Life was busy, happy and full. While my childhood family was still in pieces, I thought I had made a new experience for myself and left my old demons behind.

As the normal stress of raising kids, balancing marriage and family life hit me - I began to slip into the depths of a very dark depression. Unbeknownst to me, it was always there, lurking underneath my smile, masked with the blessings of the life that we created together. All of our dreams were coming true: we had four healthy, beautiful children, my husband had built a very successful law firm, and I had great friends and a fantastic community at Saint Mark. Yet I struggled daily, desperately asking myself why I couldn't find "happiness." I believed in God, but I didn't *know* God, His love, or His charity.

My mother-in-law, a woman of great faith and a real source of unconditional love, used to tell me to surrender everything to God, to give Him my pain, my depression, but I couldn't wrap my head around what that meant. I was losing myself, and my family was suffering with me. I tried everything I could think of to fill the hole in my heart – from shopping to exercising, to traveling, and even drinking to numb the pain. Finally, I found myself sitting in church one day, and my mother-in-law's words of wisdom came back to me... surrender your pain, and God will answer your prayers. I opened my bible to a parable in John, Chapter 4 that changed my heart and soul forever: The woman at the well.

Just as the Samaritan woman went daily to the well to have her bucket filled only to find it empty again and again, I too was filling my bucket with all the wrong things. As Jesus spoke to her, I found the answer to my painful struggles right there in this scripture. Jesus said, *"Only in me will you thirst no longer."* No one or nothing will give me the peace and life that I long for except Him. And that's when I understood what it meant to surrender fully.

I now know that if I don't take my bucket to Him when I'm scared, tired, stressed, or feeling unworthy – it will remain empty. Some days I do this better than others. But it's a daily practice that has become necessary to my life, like the air I breathe.

I remained flawed, sinful and I still struggle with life like everyone else. But I found my surrender in God. And God is always there to fill up my bucket, as many times as I ask.

Questions to Consider

1. After reading about how Erin and her brothers' lives were forever changed after their parent's divorce, does it make you realize that our modern secular society must be wrong when you hear people say things like: "The kids will be just fine?"

2. Have you ever caught yourself filling up your own bucket with the wrong things? When did this happen, and how did you realize this was wrong?

If you *forgive* others their *transgressions,* your heavenly Father will *forgive you.* But if you do not *forgive* others, neither will your Father *forgive* your *transgressions.*

- Matthew 6:14-15 -

~ Forgiveness Saves Families ~

Written by: Elza Spaedy

My mom comes from a large Catholic family. My grandparents had 14 children together. After my grandmother passed away from cancer in her early 40's, my grandfather remarried and had 7 more children with his new wife. This next life lesson came from one of her sisters. While visiting Brazil about 10 years ago, I had the opportunity to spend a lazy afternoon hanging out with one of my aunts. It was during that visit that I learned my sweet aunt had survived one of the biggest challenges in marriages today - infidelity. I was shocked to discover my uncle had cheated on her. She expressed how painful that period in her marriage was and how he had broken her heart. Being married myself for about 8 years then, I could only imagine her pain. I wanted to know how she was able to forgive him and stay married. Her answer was SO powerful that I will never forget what she said. She explained to me that if she didn't forgive him the devil would have won and destroyed her family. My aunt is a devout Catholic and was not about to let that happen! WOW... I don't know about you, but I had never heard anyone put it that way before, or since, for that matter.

She defeated the evil one because that's precisely what he wants - to destroy families. Satan knows many spouses struggling with infidelity will not be able to forgive each other. Breaking up families is his goal, but my aunt wasn't going to let evil win. Obviously what my uncle did was wrong, and I'm sure it took time for their marriage to heal, but they are still married today and growing old together surrounded by love.

As I grow in my faith, I am beginning to realize that if we are to live our Christian faith to the fullest, then we must learn to forgive each other's faults. When we pray the Lord's prayer, we say "Forgive us our trespasses, as we forgive those who trespass against us, and lead us not into temptation, but deliver us from evil." I have always loved my aunt, but that afternoon my respect and admiration for her grew to another level. She saved her marriage and family from the destruction of divorce by forgiving my uncle. What a great example of how to truly live out the gospel! If Satan was trying to destroy my family, you better believe I would fight like crazy and do whatever I could to win that battle.

Questions to Consider

1. After reading how my very wise aunt handled infidelity in her marriage, do you look at forgiveness in a new way? Do you think you could forgive your spouse after an affair, why or why not?

2. Remember, forgiveness is a gift that frees the forgiver. By letting go of these past hurts we are opening our hearts to God and all the beautiful things he wants to do in our lives. Is God calling you to forgive someone in your life that has hurt you?

Do you not know
that your body is the
temple of the Holy Spirit
who is in you,
whom you have from God,
and you are not your own?

- 1 Corinthians 6:19 -

~ Worth Waiting For ~

Written by: Ann Winkle

You are a precious daughter of God. Nothing in this world can ever take that away. You are created perfectly with everything you need to live a happy, joyful and holy life.

Growing up, I was blessed to have a very outspoken, Italian mother who reminded me of that many times. She was very passionate about Jesus, Mary and the teachings of our Catholic faith. She often said, "It's hard to be a good Catholic in our world, yet so easy if we would just follow God's plan." He designed the path so perfectly for us in every area of life.

The greatest gift my parents gave me was siblings, 10 of them to be exact, four brothers and six sisters. We are very close and are often each other's best friends and trusted advisors.

Growing up, my Mom ran a "tight ship" and developed an intense desire to protect us, especially in our teen and dating years. In our heart of hearts, we all knew that she was showing how much she cherished us, but it could sometimes be frustrating nonetheless. Friends often noticed that she was very overprotective and our social lives were always kept on a short leash. She knew the temptations of the world were everywhere, and she wanted to help us live healthy and happy lives. Once we were old enough to date, in our house that was at age 16, she taught us many lessons that I am forever grateful for now.

· Pray your rosary every day.

· Stay in the state of Grace.

· Be kind to everyone, but stand up for yourself if they start taking advantage of you.

· Always take the Blessed Mother with you.

Our Blessed Mother is the model of purity in body, heart, and soul. Because of her beautiful example, nothing seemed more important to my mom than our purity. This stems from the tradition of her upbringing, the strong teachings of our faith, and the numerous examples of saints who willingly gave up their lives to protect their purity. Mom helped me understand that God is the creator of the beautiful act of intercourse, which is meant for husbands and wives, within the confines of marriage. Giving oneself completely, body and soul is reserved for that one special person, your spouse. She presented it in such a beautiful way, illuminating God's perfect vision for me as a young woman.

"And in the end," she explained, "Every man wants someone that is pure and untouched on their wedding day. Those who work hard to protect and preserve their purity are the most treasured ones." I wanted to be a most treasured one!

Needless to say, dating one of her seven girls was not for the faint of heart. Mom's message to our dates, and to us, was often expressed in a negative "Thou Shalt Not...", But it actually voiced a very positive message: that we were special, pure, and *worth waiting for*. Often, she would give her "No Hanky-Panky" speech to every guy who started hanging around the house, which meant that she expected them to act like real gentlemen around her daughters or they would have to answer to her. Mom knew that this was a great way to separate the young men of integrity from those who were not. Often, we would complain, "Mom! That is so embarrassing. We are just friends." With her pinpoint intuition, she would smirk and respond, "That's not what *he's* thinking!" Mom raised the standards of responsibility and respect under her roof, and in doing so, she brought the best out of everyone.

We live in a world today where appropriate dating and the treasure of purity is often lost. With the internet, movies, and music encouraging open and casual sex on a daily basis, we must cling to the teachings of Jesus for guidance which leads us to lasting love and happiness. If we follow the proper order of God's plan, we will encounter joy and contentment. If we stray and design our own path, or do things "out of order"' away from God's plan, we will eventually discover pain and sorrow.

Consider this analogy. Our sexuality is like a fire. When the fire is carefully built, managed and protected in the fireplace where it belongs, it is beautiful, warm, comforting, romantic, and mesmerizing. It provides much-needed warmth and the ability to nourish. Yet, when a spark from that same fire shoots out of the fireplace, it suddenly burns out of control, charing your home causing great anxiety, injury and sometimes even death.

If you've allowed a spark out of the fireplace, it's never too late to stomp it out and rebuild that safe, warm fire again. You are a precious daughter of God, and definitely worth waiting for.

Questions to Consider

1. Where in your life can you increase the purity of mind, body, and soul? Are the television shows and movies your family is watching promoting Christian values? What about the music?

2. How can you teach healthy boundaries to your daughters, so they understand and appreciate the gift of purity?

Now if we are children, then we are *heirs* —heirs of God and co-heirs with Christ, if indeed we share in his *sufferings* in order that we may also share in his *glory*. I consider that our *present sufferings* are not worth comparing with the *glory* that will be revealed in us.

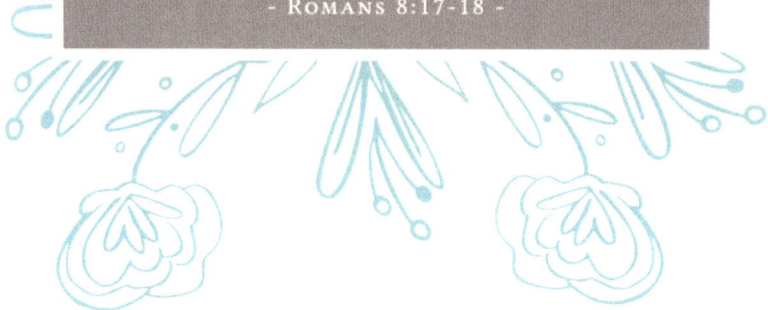

- Romans 8:17-18 -

~ Trusting His Plan ~

Written by: Alexandra Stanley

Growing up in a Catholic household I, along with my 5 siblings, have been shown what it means to develop a close relationship with our Lord, trust His plan, and be the best example of Christ's light that we can. I can't think of a Sunday that we didn't attend Mass, a time we weren't reminded to thank God for our meal before we enjoyed it, or a Christmas that we didn't take time to remember its true meaning- the birth of our Christ. While I grew up learning more about my faith and eventually accepting these beliefs as my own, it wasn't until my high school and early college years that I truly learned what the most faithful life looked like. A large part of this was because of the example my mother showed us.

My mother didn't grow up Catholic, she actually grew up Episcopalian. However, after marrying my Dad, and learning more about the faith, she decided to convert to Catholicism. She became one of the most important people in my life as I learned more about my faith and had to make decisions for myself. While I was preparing for the Sacrament of Confirmation, my faith wasn't nearly as strong, and I didn't always understand some of the things my mom would talk to me about or want me to do. For example, she started sending me to Life Teen at my church, which I didn't enjoy at first. This was most likely because I hadn't yet developed a close personal relationship with God. But my mom knew that I would and that she just had to be the example God asks us all to be for our children. I also remember a time when she started bringing up Jesus and His messages in more conversations than not. She strived to make connections between things we experienced and how God wanted us to handle these situations. Whether it be an internal struggle, something that happened at school, or how we were treating our siblings. It's funny because as I was growing in my own faith, I saw hers growing stronger and deeper as well. Looking back, I couldn't be more thankful for her strong influence and the excellent example of a Catholic life that she led.

Along with the craziness of raising 6 kids, my mom faced her own struggles, as she was diagnosed with cancer when I was in 4th grade, and it became an even harder battle my sophomore year of high school. Even though she was going through this difficult time, I never saw her struggle or stray from her faith. In fact, I witnessed her relationship with God become stronger. I would come home and sit on her bed, or come back from college and just hear her talk more about God's purpose and plan for us all here on earth. He has a plan for us all, and I know that His plan for my mom was just exactly what she did and how she lived her life. She was a great evangelist for my family. My mother lit up any room she walked into with Christ's light. Discussion of the homily and readings, and making connections to things that we experienced throughout the week became even more common as I got older. I was amazed by her strong and steadfast faith. Even though she was going through a physically trying time, she never let it show. She had a beautiful smile on her face and continued to keep her relationship with God as the most important thing in her life. This was closely followed by how she cared for my dad, my siblings, her family, and her friends.

I know that watching my mom's relationship with God foster and strengthen was what brought me closer to God myself. It inspired me to continue asking questions, learning more, and attending Mass even when I went off to college. My mom's passing my sophomore year of high school was extremely difficult for my family. It took a lot for me to get back on my path, and I am still getting there. However, my relationship with God and trusting that it was somehow all part of His plan has helped get me through. I am so thankful for the base of faith that my mom created for us, and how she led us to make it our own. The most important thing is that your faith is your own because no two relationships with God can be the same. God has a plan for each and every one of us. While my mom's sickness was hard on her and all of our family, I can't help but know that it was a large part of her path in growing in her faith and helping my siblings and I learn as much from her as we could. I am so thankful for all she taught me, as I know it has helped me grow into the person I am today. While I am still very sad that my mom had to leave us 2 years ago, I know that she was fulfilled and left in peace because of the person she was, how she followed God, and the tremendous Catholic example she passed on to us, her children. I know that she followed God's path allowing her a lifetime of eternal happiness with Him.

I am incredibly thankful for the guidance that my mom gave and still gives me. To this day I see her in the little things, and I feel her pushing me in specific directions. I still feel these urges that a particular choice is what she would show me how to do if she were still here with me. And this only reassures me that God is right here with me too. He may have taken her from earth, but she will never really leave us. The suffering we went through helped us all grow stronger in our relationships with Him, and that is the most important thing of all. Thinking about everything she taught me and the love she showed always puts a smile on my face. I can't wait for the day that I get to pass on the Catholic faith in the same way my mom did, and I only hope to show my children as great of an example as she showed us.

Questions to Consider

1. What can you do today to nurture and develop a closer personal relationship with our Lord?

2. What was the most important lesson you have learned from an influential woman in your life? Have you passed that lesson on to others?

THERE IS AN

appointed time for everything,

AND A TIME FOR EVERY AFFAIR

UNDER THE HEAVENS.

- ECCLESIASTES 3:1 -

~ Christ Is Counting on You ~

Written by: Mary Meixner

(Jennifer Creter's Mom)

When did you last set aside a prolonged period to reflect, rejuvenate and rest in God? Perhaps years ago. Maybe never. Most of us long for time alone to think, pray, contemplate, meditate, learn and listen to God speaking directly to us. A spiritual retreat can be the answer. Of course, there are a myriad of reasons why scheduling time away for yourself is impractical, but if you truly think about it, you will realize with some planning, it is not impossible. Is God calling you?

A retreat positively changed my life and, I believe, my unborn child's. Many years ago, I accepted an invitation to participate in a Cursillo, an intense three-day course in Christianity. The weekend was held at a Franciscan friary in Cincinnati, Ohio with 64 women from many area parishes in attendance. Upon arrival the first day, we were ushered into a large gymnasium-like room and assigned our bunks. The sight of 64 cots lined up barrack style gave me pause. Being five months pregnant, I thought, "How can I possibly manage to sleep in a room with so many women?"

In the chapel at 8 o'clock that evening, we met a Franciscan priest who would serve as one of the retreat leaders. He told us, "I don't know why you believe you are here, but I'm certain you were called by a higher power." He explained that all would become clearer as the weekend progressed. He also told us that we would leave with a renewed sense of direction and purpose in life. We learned that the motto of the Cursillo was "Christ is Counting on You." He instructed us to ponder that overwhelming thought in silence for the next 12 hours. Imagine 64 women, who have never met, spending the night in close quarters and not able to talk.

The following morning we were divided into groups of eight. After listening to presentations by laywomen and religious, we shared thoughts on topics such as women in the church, sacraments, obstacles to grace, leadership, and study. Throughout each day, we listened, talked, sang, ate, prayed, cried, laughed and built community. I have no doubt that the Holy Spirit was with us filling our hearts with love and showering us with His grace.

On Sunday morning, the third day, the liturgy was a happy and uplifting celebration. As we sang and prayed, faces beamed and tears of joy flowed. The time came to head back to our homes and families. It was difficult to say goodbye to many new sisters-in-Christ. But, we promised God and each other that we would take what we learned during those 72 hours and work toward making the world a more loving, peaceful place. For me, the afterglow of those three days carried over into the "fourth day" which is the rest of one's life.

Several months after the Cursillo, I was blessed by the birth of a healthy baby girl, Mary Jennifer. I sincerely believe that both she and I together benefited from the outpouring of God's grace and the abundant love which flowed unceasingly during that retreat. Today, she is a beautiful, spirit-filled woman open to recognizing and appreciating the gifts generously given by our gracious God. She continuously embraces the opportunity to do her part in making her faith community at St. Mark a more welcoming, loving and peaceful place. I am grateful, and I am proud.

You never know what God has planned for you. Surely, there is an upcoming retreat that will fit your schedule and fulfill your needs. Seek it out. Put hesitation aside. Give yourself this gift. Make space for God. Christ IS counting on YOU!

Prayer to the Holy Spirit: Come Holy Spirit, fill the hearts of your faithful and kindle in them the fire of your love. Send forth your Spirit, and they shall be created. And you shall renew the face of the earth.

O, God, who by the light of the Holy Spirit, did instruct the hearts of the faithful, grant by that same Holy Spirit we may be truly wise and ever enjoy His consolations, Through Christ Our Lord, Amen.

Questions to Consider

1. Have you ever felt called by God to take on a spiritual experience that expanded your prayer life and increased your knowledge of the Catholic faith?

2. If you've never been to a retreat, would you consider attending one? If not, what's holding you back?

As each one has received a *gift,* use it to

serve one another

as good stewards of God's varied grace.

- 1 Peter 4:10 -

~ Using Your God-given Gifts ~

Written by: Caitlin Bristow

I come from a line of artistic, creative women, who passed along their love of making things to me. On a daily basis, I feel the desire to be creative, but like many moms, I often wonder how these God-given interests and passions fit into my day-to-day life. In these moments, I'm so thankful I can look back at the example of my grandma and mom because their faith and influence continue to guide me.

Growing up, I watched my grandma paint in a simple space she set up in her basement, with boxes and boxes of acrylic paints surrounding her as she made whatever inspired her. Christmas ornaments, decorative pumpkins, birdhouses, crew neck sweatshirts. (Allow me to assure you that in the early 90s, those hand-painted sweatshirts were all the rage.) She had eight kids, tons of grandkids and people coming and going out of her house at all times of the day. But what did she make time for? Creating things for the joy of it.

And then there was my own mom, who with her four kids and a full-time job, had a full plate. She taught more religious education classes than I could ever count. She was the "Elementary School Fun Fair Mom" and famously the "Cross Country Meet Mom" who cheered for every kid in the race.

And between all the goings-on of our active family, she found ways to bring her very artistic giftings into our daily lives. She wrote a cookbook. She developed recipes and designed covers and sold them at craft shows. She hand-smocked dresses and sewed pretty much everything, from princess costumes to pillowcases to pajamas to puppets. She painted birthday signs, block party banners, backdrops for Children's Liturgy lessons. She, like her mom, had an artistic flair that did not hit pause when my siblings and I arrived. If anything, she channeled it in new ways, bringing her own flavor of fun and creativity into motherhood. She brought beauty into our home in many ways that I'm appreciating on a whole new level now that I have two kids of my own.

So what does this mean for my life today? God is calling me to bring all the gifts He's provided to the motherhood table. He is asking me to create with joy amidst the busyness of everyday life, remembering our great Creator as I do it. Sometimes that's finger painting with a toddler, and sometimes that's lettering art prints after the kids are sound asleep. It all counts.

Your passions and strengths will likely be different, but whatever God has given you, share it with your family. He will use these gifts to bring Him glory, and our families will get to watch with wonder and delight.

"Artists of the world, may your many different paths all lead to that infinite Ocean of beauty where wonder becomes awe, exhilaration, unspeakable joy. May you be guided and inspired by the mystery of the Risen Christ, whom the Church in these days contemplates with joy. May the Blessed Virgin Mary be with you always: she is the "tota pulchra" portrayed by countless artists, whom Dante contemplates among the splendours of Paradise as "beauty that was joy in the eyes of all the other saints."

Letter to Artists, Saint John Paul II

Questions to Consider

1. As Caitlin said, creativity can be expressed in hundreds of different ways. Think back to a time when you felt pure joy and happiness while creating something. What was it, and when?

2. How can you use the beautiful gifts God has given you to bring your family closer together? What about your church community?

Trust IN THE LORD WITH ALL YOUR *heart,* ON YOUR OWN INTELLIGENCE DO NOT RELY; IN ALL YOUR WAYS BE *mindful* OF HIM, AND HE WILL *make straight* YOUR PATHS.

- PROVERBS 3:5-6 -

~ When I'm Afraid, I Will Trust in Him ~

Written by: Kristyn Keenan

The Church's teaching of Natural Family Planning is the reason I am a Catholic today. I grew up in a Protestant home and was enrolled in education at a local Baptist school. We Protestants felt intellectually superior to Catholics in all areas of our religious life except for one: I was completely ignorant on the topic of contraception. As a young Christian woman, the natural understanding was to date a man, get engaged, see an OB/GYN to get on birth control and then get married and enjoy life as husband and wife. My future husband, Brian, and I were always in sync, this progression included. I spent about a year on several different birth control pills trying to find the one that worked for my body. I never liked the way I felt on the hormones. Later, I would switch to the patch. The patch seemed to be the best option because I was traveling a lot for my job at the time and I thought it would make my life easier. That was the turning point. Being on the patch was a hormonal shock to my system. I had so many negative side effects, and my disdain of the medication grew even stronger. It eventually got to the point that I had decided to bring up the idea to my husband, Brian: ceasing hormonal birth control altogether. I just KNEW he would say no. This was in 2012, and we weren't in a place to start having children yet. But I wouldn't know until I brought it up to him. **I was afraid, but I trusted in Him.**

The Holy Spirit...who knew that at the same time I was going through this huge internal struggle, the Lord was also preparing Brian's heart in the same direction (neither of us was being directed toward the Catholic church at this point, or so we thought). One night at dinner, I remember thinking I was just going to drop the bomb, "I don't want to be on birth control anymore!" I cringed waiting for his sarcastic "Yeah, right!" But he lovingly responded with, "Okay." He spent that evening watching me cry and listening as I described to him how I hated being on this medication. I didn't feel like me, and I knew there had to be another option that would work for us. Coincidently, Brian had just finished reading an article by Elizabeth Anscombe called "Contraception and Chastity," about this very same issue. He talked with his best friend Adam, who was in the process of converting to Catholicism and told him about our conversation. Adam encouraged us to look into Natural Family Planning. "But that's with the Catholic Church," I said. Brian explained that we wouldn't be joining the church; it would just require taking a class. **I was afraid, but I trusted in Him.**

This class was like none other! My mind was repeatedly blown away at the biology I was learning. MY biology! Things that my body was doing that I had always recognized, but never knew why. I was learning about when I was ovulating, which was not when doctors were telling me I was ovulating. I learned that because I ovulated later in my cycle, I would have some issues with conception and keeping a pregnancy, a devastating realization at the time. The couple who taught our NFP class was so kind and recommended a practice in Fairfax, VA that was NFP friendly. It was a Catholic OB/GYN office called Tepeyac Family Center, and they were absolutely from the Lord. They immediately recognized my cycle issues and knew how to help us. During my first pregnancy with Grace in early 2013, I was given progesterone to correct my hormone levels and needed to be very careful during the first trimester. I remember being on the way to the airport for a business trip, getting a call from my doctor who told me I needed to get on the progesterone immediately because I was at high risk of miscarrying. **I was afraid, but I trusted in Him.**

Our daughter Grace was born healthy and thriving. We were happy and loved being parents. However, I didn't realize it at the time, but my husband and I were being torn apart. For Brian, practicing NFP meant real conversion. Up to this point, his interest in the Catholic church was entirely intellectual. He was reading a ton of books and having great conversations with Adam weekly. The Holy Spirit was moving in him, in ways I didn't see. Brian wanted to convert, and he shared this with me – a lot. How could the Lord be leading him in a direction and not also be leading me? How could we join a church in which we didn't know a single person? How could we tell our families that we were leaving the church in which they had lovingly and faithfully raised us? I wasn't ready to come to grips with these questions and resented that Brian was heading in a direction that I wasn't. Graciously, Brian gave me the gift of time. He said he would give me five years to come to a decision, then he would convert without me. I told him I only needed two. **I was afraid, but I trusted in Him.**

Natural Family Planning was how our children were brought into the world. I use the word "planning" loosely. We were open to what God wanted for us and believed that we should always be receptive to having children. But our third born, Rosalind, was the only child we truly planned. We specifically prayed for her and intentionally conceived her. For me, it was the first time I could see the Lord's fulfillment of His plan since I had the initial thought to quit birth control. In March 2018, I told Brian I was ready to come home to the Catholic Church. I had finally seen the beauty of His creation, through my own body, and I desired to be faithful to His blessings. We joined the church in April 2018, and He has continued to show Himself faithful to us and, with love, answer all my questions. Now I'm actually looking forward to those sometimes scary prepubescent years with my daughters. I can't wait to teach Grace and Rosalind (and any future daughters) the beauty in which God created their bodies. Those years are so mysterious to a child and can be just as scary for a parent. But these lessons also apply to my son, Alasdair. Males should grow up understanding the internal beauty of a female and why God designed her the way He did. As I lead them through those years, **I will be afraid, but I will trust in Him.**

All of this brings me to Pope Paul VI predictions more than 50 years ago when he wrote his beautiful encyclical "Humanae Vitae." He also emphasized that the Catholic Church calls couples to marriages that are free, total, faithful and fruitful. Here are just a few examples of what he warned would happen if the world accepted birth control as part of normal, daily life:

1. **The Objectification of Women-** Pope Paul VI commented, "Not much experience is needed to be fully aware of human weakness and to understand that human beings- especially the young, who are so exposed to temptation, need incentives to keep the moral law, and it's an evil thing to make it easy for them to break the law." He also wrote, "Another fact that gives cause for alarm is that a man who has grown accustomed to the use of contraceptive methods may forget the reverence due to a woman, and disregard her physical and emotional equilibrium - reducing her to a mere instrument for the satisfaction of his own desires."

2. **Marriage under attack-** "It's to be anticipated that not everyone will easily accept this particular teaching." Pope Paul VI reflected, "There is too much outcry against the voice of the Church that is intensified by modern means of communication. But it comes as no surprise to our Mother Church that she, no less than her divine Founder, is destined to be a sign of contradiction."

Today we live in a world that has redefined marriage according to popular opinion. "Mandating marriage redefinition is a tragic error that harms the common good and most vulnerable among us, especially children," Archbishop Joseph Kurtz of Louisville, Kentucky wrote in 2015. "The law has a duty to support every child's basic right to be raised, whenever possible, by his or her married mother and father in a stable home."

3. **Unfaithfulness in marriage-** "Responsible men can become more deeply convinced of the truth of the doctrine laid down by the Church on this issue if they reflect on the consequences of methods and plans for artificial birth control," Pope Paul VI commented upon the release of the pill in the 1960s. "Let them first consider how easily this course of action could

open wide the way for marital infidelity and a general lowering of moral standards." The pope's words seem highly prophetic given the 2015 release of over **37 million birth control users** names and identities from the company Ashley Madison. The website specialized in providing environments for spousal infidelity.

Questions to Consider

1. We know natural family planning works, but what are some of the other key benefits for a woman's entire body, mind, and soul? How can we teach teens about the beauty of their bodies and God's plan for sexuality?

2. After reading about the Catholic Church's teaching on contraceptives and about Pope Paul VI prophetic predictions about what would happen if we accepted birth control into our lives, do you have a different opinion on the topic?

THESE COMMANDMENTS THAT I GIVE YOU

TODAY ARE TO BE ON YOUR HEARTS.

Impress them on your children.

TALK ABOUT THEM WHEN YOU *sit*

AT HOME AND WHEN YOU *walk* ALONG

THE ROAD, WHEN YOU *lie down* AND

WHEN YOU *get up.*

- DEUTERONOMY 6:6-9 -

~ Families Sharing Their Faith ~

Written by: Elza Spaedy

My mom grew up in a devout Catholic family, and one of her dreams was to pass her love of Catholicism on to her children. Unfortunately for us, her dream was not our reality back then because my dad was not Catholic. Not only was he not religious, but he also didn't care for the Catholic Church. When I was about 8 or 9 years old, our weekly visits to Mass abruptly ended. I had always assumed it was because my dad pressured my mom to stop going. While putting together this book, I knew I needed to understand what happened. Why was religion absent in our lives? I had to ask my mom some tough questions, and thankfully she was willing to answer. My suspicions were confirmed, and as the head of our household, my dad made the decision that would change all of our lives. Even though we stopped going to mass, by the grace of God the seeds my mom planted in me as a child were already rooted. I was Catholic in my heart and my soul. Years later, when I was yearning for God, I found myself back in His church and heard God's gentle voice say to me "You are to close that gap that your mom was coerced into opening." One of my daily prayers is that David and I will always be faithful to God and His Church and that our children will continue to practice the Catholic faith in their families.

When I was a teenager, I remember my mom telling me to marry a man that shares my faith. She understood how important that was and wanted to spare me the heartache and disappointment that comes from being in a marriage without God at the center. I listened carefully to her advice and wisdom, and when I met my husband David, I knew my prayers had been answered.

I have been blessed with a wonderful man in David, and we have gone to church and prayed together ever since we started dating. We also know that God comes first and that it's our responsibility to raise the next generation of faithful Catholics. We take that responsibility very seriously, and I find myself passing on my mother's words of wisdom to my kids. Our most important job as parents is to teach our children about God and to live the Gospel by our example. And those phrases that we hear so often today like: "I don't need to go to church to know God" or "I'm not religious, but I'm spiritual" are all part of the Devil's lies. As our children's first teachers, it is our job to help them become saints. Whom they choose to spend their lives with will have a significant impact on their spiritual journey and ultimately their salvation. It's my prayer that more parents will stress just how crucial it is to have a spouse who will support and encourage a lifelong relationship with our Lord and Savior.

Questions to Consider

1. After reading about how my mom had to make the tough choice to walk away from her Catholic faith after being pressured by my dad, do you think you'll be more inclined to talk to your children (starting at a very young age) about the importance of praying for a spouse who shares their faith?

2. Attending daily Mass has taken my faith life to a much deeper level. Have you ever thought about adding a daily mass to your weekly schedule? Why or why not?

COME ALL YOU WHO LABOR

AND ARE BURDENED,

and I will give you rest.

- MATTHEW 11:28 -

~ Learning to Rest in Him ~

Written by: Kristin Winkle Beck

The popular cliché, "Work hard, play hard," was my mantra for many years. I was born into a family of small business owners in a tiny Midwestern town. Hard work was practically part of my DNA. I was taught to work hard at a young age and applied it to whichever season of life I experienced. As a student, my years of efforts inside and outside the classroom paid off with good grades, sports trophies, and getting accepted to my first choice of universities. I enrolled in college five hundred miles away from everyone I knew. I had to work even harder to re-establish my reputation. I was in a more rigorous academic setting and worked a part-time job to help cover my living expenses on campus. Every time I came through a particularly stressful or hardworking season, I saw the fruits of my labor. I achieved the desired grades and earned enough money to cover the semester's expenses. As my college career came to an end, my successes there landed me an impressive job in corporate America. I was finally joining the real world, but now the REAL hard work would begin.

At twenty-two years old, I was a new manager responsible for the performance of twenty people in a large financial services corporation. Eager to continue my track record of success, I attended training seminars and sought the best practices from seasoned managers. I even flexed my schedule between first and second shifts, many nights getting home from work around 12:30 am and going back to the office the next day before 8am. There was little talk of rest and even less of it in my daily reality.

For the next fifteen years, I would work 50-60 hours a week, volunteer to take on additional assignments, and offer to fill in gaps for my colleagues and the company. I was blessed to work for companies with generous vacation benefits. The sad reality was I worked extra hard preparing to leave my work behind (which I rarely ever did), and then worked even harder upon my return from vacation to catch up on emails and projects that piled up while I was away. I planned fun vacations with family and friends, but, I rarely allowed myself to unplug from emails or meetings entirely.

I continued to climb the corporate ladder changing companies and moving around the South. Each successive promotion brought more responsibility, more extended hours, heavier workloads, and higher stress. I would work tirelessly for weeks (and sometimes months) on end and then crash on a Saturday or long weekend, desperately trying to catch up on sleep or hibernate in my house to try to replenish my energy. I was exhausted, and the opportunities to play and rest became even rarer. I was working myself into someone I no longer recognized. My attention to my physical health had diminished, despite the fact I knew it would help me manage my stress. I would often joke with friends if it couldn't be delivered to my house or picked up through a drive-through window, I didn't eat it. I gained weight and lost energy. I was prioritizing my work above all else.

After enduring a painful divorce that completely blindsided me, I found myself in my mid-thirties emotionally exhausted and alone. While I had always been a Christian, I began to feel God's presence in an entirely new way. I truly developed a personal relationship with Jesus and leaned upon Him for guidance and direction in my life. I was still stubbornly charging forward and working hard to provide for myself financially. This continued for a few more years until I felt God asking me to allow Him to direct my professional life too. He wanted ALL of me—my relationships, my hobbies, my health, and my career. Work had always been something I felt good about, and it filled me with a sense of accomplishment. I started to feel disconnected and disenchanted. I began to incorporate prayers about my professional challenges into my daily time with God. He would always answer me with a scripture verse or a devotional that was exactly what my soul needed that day.

For two years, I wrestled with dissatisfaction and uncertainty about my professional future. I came across a blog post about observing the Sabbath. I started to explore this concept and read what the Bible had to say on this topic. God doesn't suggest we take a break; He commands us to do it. In the creation story in Genesis 2, God rested from all the work He had done on the seventh day. And He blessed the seventh day BECAUSE He rested. I began to put my learnings into practice. I set aside Sundays as a day without obligations. I would attend church and then use this day for activities that recharged me. Occasionally I would meet a friend for lunch or go see a movie. I didn't use Sundays to do any household chores or commit to any activities that didn't bring me joy or re-energize me. This small step was difficult for this goal-oriented achiever who was always worrying about my efficiency and ever-growing "to-do" list, but it started to make a difference in my life.

I also starting visiting a local retreat house called Well of Mercy for more extended periods of rest. It was during my weekend trips there with no agenda, no commitment or obligations that I began to really sense God wanted me to live differently. While on retreat, I slept when I was tired, ate when I was hungry and simply had the time to just BE. I heard God in my prayers in the chapel, following a nap in a hammock, and on the pages of my Bible while rocking in a chair on the front porch. He was insisting that I stay/abide/remain/be still where I was in my job, but I felt God leading me to explore opportunities to use my gifts and talents to serve others when I wasn't working.

As I began to volunteer in a variety of new ways, I continued to pray daily for God to change my work circumstances, seeking His wisdom for my career. Then He answered me with clear guidance - "REST." "Come to me all you who labor and are burdened, and I will give you rest." This verse, taken from Matthew 11:28, appeared to me repeatedly in a variety of places. It was as if I couldn't outrun this verse. "Rest, Lord? You want me to rest? I'm already resting on Sundays," I whispered in my prayer. I wanted a new job, I didn't want to rest. I began to research sabbaticals and evaluate all the practical things, especially finances that would have to be considered to take a year off. He knew I was struggling with this idea of rest, so He brought me to a ten-day Bible study on the word "rest" while I was on vacation. Following those 10 days, His plan became crystal clear. I was supposed to turn my sabbath into a sabbatical.

About a month later, I surrendered and gave notice to my employer that I was leaving. I knew that God was calling me out of the workforce and out of my comfort zone. I was to trust Him with my future and my career fully. During my sabbatical, I also stepped down from volunteer commitments and reconnected with loved ones. I planned trips, read books, occasionally binge-watched Netflix, and marveled at the blessings God bestowed upon me. He gave me a great appreciation for who He is and who I am to Him. And during that year, He also revealed a new vocation to me when it was time to return to the workforce. I realized that if I hadn't taken the time to rest and be still, I might never have been able to discern His wisdom for my life.

As I re-entered the workforce, I was more conscious of the need to prioritize rest among the other demands of life. I recently read a quote in Priscilla Shirer's book *Breathe, Making Room for Sabbath* that said, "Rest was the capstone of creation, and without it, the universe would be incomplete." How ironic to consider that our work, our lives, and all of God's creation are not complete without rest.

Questions to Consider

1. If God Himself rested, why do you struggle with or feel guilty about resting?

2. What specific steps can you take to incorporate rest into your hectic and busy lifestyle?

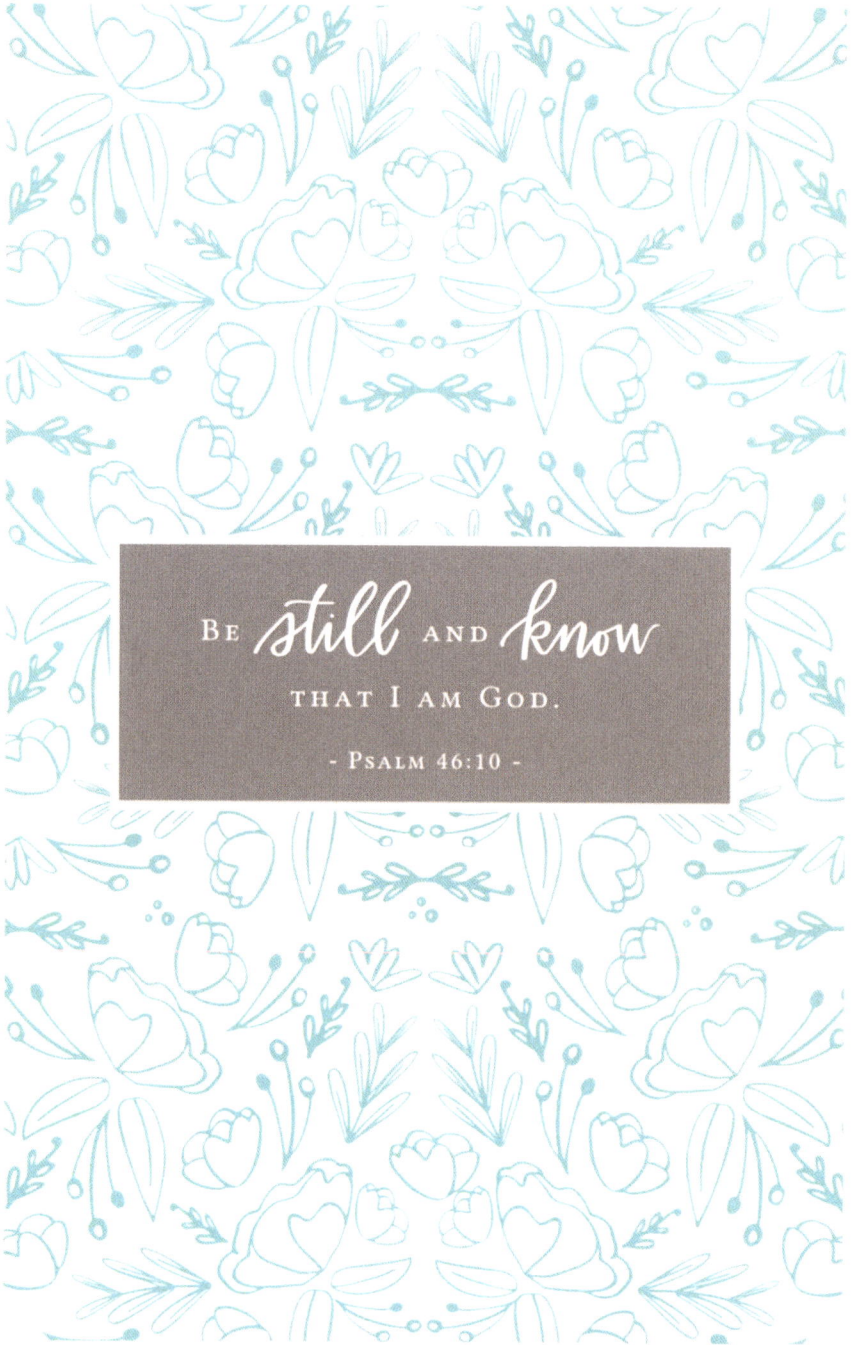

BE *still* AND *know* THAT I AM GOD.

- PSALM 46:10 -

~ Finding Peace and Joy in Doing God's Will~

Written by: Sarah Miller

I was raised Catholic, a lukewarm Catholic at best. One hour Mass on Sunday, check. That was all I was giving to God. I didn't know any better at the time. Growing up, I was told I could be anything I wanted. Confidence quickly became pride.

As an athlete, I ran 10 miles a day. I competed in events where world records were broken. I wasn't the one breaking the record, but that was the level I was competing. As a young professional, I became a National Account Manager at age 23. Yay me! Next, I was promoted to Vice President of National Account Sales at 33. Good job, Sarah!

Back to my faith commitment, or lack thereof, I was still going to Mass one hour a week on Sundays. I always heard about suffering and "offering it up," but what did that mean? Offer it up?! I was about to find out the hard way. After experiencing various symptoms for years, at age 31, I was officially diagnosed with Multiple Sclerosis. No more running and eventually no more working. Often, I would be homebound and hooked up to an IV 24 hours a day for a week at a time.

Luckily in my 20's I fell in love with a wonderful man, got married and together we have two beautiful children. I once thought I would have 12 kids. My diagnosis gave me the rude awakening that I was not in control. Because of my illness, we were struggling financially. I knew my place as wife and mom, but what else was my purpose?

Out of desperation, I did something quite uncharacteristic of myself, I invited God into my life. Praying became life-changing for me. The Holy Spirit inspired me to pray for a priest I met when I was a child. In God's divine wisdom, He took my focus off of me and my worries. Initially, it didn't go over well. I wasn't sure how to pray for someone I hadn't seen in decades. Don't you have to know someone's needs to know how to pray for him? Well, apparently you don't, because God knew what this priest needed. So after I questioned God, He did quite the impossible. He allowed me to experience this poor priest's suffering. Not physical pain, but deep emotional suffering. My heart felt so broken for him, and I promised God that I would never question Him again. While praying for this priest for hours, I realized how much God truly loved him despite his sins. It was days later when I learned this priest was in prison for misconduct. Once upon a time, I would have judged him, but all I could feel was love for him...God's love.

As my disease progressed, the IV's became necessary. It was challenging and uncomfortable trying to sleep with an IV hooked up to my arm. Many nights I would wake up at 2 or 3 in the morning, and that's when God would show me priests who needed my prayers. Sometimes I knew the reasons why, but most of the time I didn't. I felt God's powerful love for each and every one them. They were His chosen sons, and they were hurting. As we all know, priests are human, and humans aren't perfect. Neither am I. And to be honest, suffering from this disease has been really hard...even harder before I found purpose in it. During the earlier days, I became familiar with Psalm 46:10 "*Be Still and Know That I am God.*" I have quite literally clung to that verse.

Even though I did not personally know the majority of priests I prayed for, there was one instance I was awakened and inspired to pray for a young seminarian whom I had met only once. The inspiration was so intense that I spent the rest of the night praying for him. The next day, to my shock I got an email from this young seminarian. I didn't even remember exchanging contact information with him. He began the email "Dear Madam," and then asked for my prayers.

These inspirations have gone on for over a decade. God's love poured through me as I prayed for these priests, and my own joy and peace increased. I knew I was right where I was supposed to be. Sure my weakness and pain were growing as the disease was progressing, but I had finally accepted it. More importantly than receiving it, I saw value in it! If I had been out running 10 miles a day plus working in a big career, patting myself on the back, I never would have slowed down long enough to hear God. If the only thing to grab my attention was a chronic disease, then praise be His name.

There was a particular seminarian I prayed for 10+ years. It was that long because somewhere in the midst of his formation, he left the seminary. I so clearly remember Our Lord showing me that I am going to pray and offer my suffering for him. And that's precisely what I did. In God's goodness, the seminarian returned to his formation. Two days before he was ordained I had a 2 ½ hour MRI scan of my brain and spine. At the start of the scan, I began praying "Lord this is all for the seminarian, I'm not going to waste a minute." I spent the entire time in prayer. Two days later, I had the honor of attending his ordination, where he prostrated himself before the altar, dedicating his life to God. I cannot imagine anything more worthy.

So my life of prayer and suffering is focused on praying for priests, specifically for seminarians who hear God's call. At the same time I'm praying, I know the evil one is trying to pull them away by tempting them with the pleasures of this world. It's an obvious battle.

The reason I have joy and peace today is that I know I'm doing God's will. I have a vibrant prayer life, and I go to daily Mass to receive Jesus' body and blood in the Eucharist every chance I get. Finally, when I reflect on "offering it up" I can't help but think about Jesus himself who made the most significant offering possible...His life! And how He now permits us to offer up our little struggles, and unite them with his, for love of him and for the whole world. Yay God!

Questions to Consider

1. As Sarah illustrates so beautifully, when we pray for others we get the focus off of ourselves. Have you ever thought about offering up your sufferings in prayer for others?

2. What are some of the ways that God may be calling you to support our priests and seminarians? Are you nurturing the idea of a priestly vocation within your own family?

FIND YOUR *delight* IN THE *Lord* WHO WILL GIVE YOU YOUR *heart's desire.*

- PSALM 37:4 -

~ Authentic Femininity ~

Written by: Olivia Shingledecker

As women, the desires of our hearts are vulnerable places where many lies creep in. As a young woman, I have many desires: the desire to be accepted, to have real friendships, to be pursued by a young man, to chase my dreams, to create beauty in the world - and the list goes on.

I can remember being in eighth grade, feeling these desires surface in my life, and not knowing what to do with them. Then I had the beautiful opportunity to attend a day retreat for young women at the invitation of a young high school girl in love with Christ and her faith. On that retreat, the priest explained everything about those womanly desires that were surfacing in my heart. He described the fundamental differences between men and women - that women are called to motherhood and men to fatherhood. He beautifully outlined the desires of a woman's heart and how they affect her relationship with God and others.

That retreat was the beginning of my exploration of what it means to be a young Catholic woman. Since then, I have learned that as women, we are the model and standard of the human race. I was particularly intrigued by St. John Paul II in his concept of the "feminine genius." He talked about a woman's unique gifts of receptivity, sensitivity, generosity, and maternity. My personal favorite of these gifts is a woman's receptivity. As women, our bodies were created to be open to and receive life. This external reality points to the internal reality of our souls. Because of our extraordinary ability to receive, we are the model of how all humans should be receptive to God. Because we are the model of humanity's relationship with God, we set the standards for our society.

Our culture and the modern world wants to make a woman only as valuable as her body, her career, her looks, her emotional toughness, and her sex appeal. Faced with these lies from society, pressures from our peers, and our own struggles in our faith journeys - it can be easy to squash our true feminine desires. I experienced this in the years following that initial retreat on the feminine genius. As time progressed, I started to get worn out and forgot the beauty of being a woman.

The pressures of high school made me anxious and worried. I was often faced with the choice of lowering my standards, especially regarding modesty, because of peer pressure. I was frustrated in my search for authentic, Christ-centered friendships. I often desired the attention of a young man, but no one asked me out. And of course, there were my changing hormones that often got the best of my self-control and emotions.

Ladies, I want you to know that as a senior in high school these are things I *still* struggle with. But what I've come to realize is that all of these realities - the outside pressures and our own struggles - are all tools the evil one uses to squash those deepest desires of our hearts.

In a moment of crying out to the Lord in prayer, I remember asking Him to take away my womanly desires for love and motherhood because it didn't seem like they would ever be fulfilled the way I wanted. The Lord gently made it clear to me that taking away these desires would actually be taking away an essential part of my womanhood.

The desires of our hearts are not wrong, as we would sometimes believe. My wish for true friendship was something the Lord wanted to fulfill after I had become best friends with Him. My desire to be pursued by a young man was something that Jesus Himself wanted to fulfill by pursuing my heart. My hope to be accepted by dressing like everyone else was replaced by the more profound desire to save my body for true love in my future vocation. My desire to be a mother was fulfilled when I realized that I could bear Christ to the world by mothering everyone I meet. And when my crazy emotions would manifest themselves, it became an invitation for me to be receptive to God.

The Lord wants to heal our desires and for us to be free in Him. We have to constantly, even daily refresh our hearts on the truth of our identity as beloved women of God. We forget that in our femininity we were designed to image humanity's relationship with God, and even to image God Himself. So much of the secret to joy is accepting and deeply living our feminine gifts and making sense of our desires in light of the Faith.

How do we do this? By allowing the truth and reality that Christ is our ultimate desire to sink deeply into our souls. The primary way I am able to turn my heart back to the Lord is by encountering Him in Scripture and in Eucharistic Adoration. Just sitting and being with Christ in His Word and in His real presence transforms my hurting and straying heart. This is a practice I have to continually turn to, as I face new struggles in my life and soul as a young Catholic woman. Christ Himself is pursuing our hearts. All he asks of us is that we find in Him all of our hearts' desires. That is the secret to and the heart of authentic femininity.

Questions to Consider

1. Who are those women who model authentic femininity for you?

2. When have you been tempted to squash the desires of your heart? How can you concretely surrender them to Christ?

You are *precious* and *honored* in my sight, and *I love you.*

- ISAIAH 43:4A -

~ Allowing God to Pursue My Heart ~

Written by: Katie Miller

People seem to have a hard time believing that chastity and purity are still attainable in the modern age. Social media, movies, music - all of these portray the normality of the hookup culture. Love is devalued to the point of mere physicality and sexual gratification. As a young teenager, I started witnessing the fruits of this culture in many of my friends. They fawned over each guy they crossed paths with; there was a new "love of my life" every week. Personally, I found their behavior to be a bit embarrassing and in my attempt to keep myself from this embarrassment I prayed to God that he would "protect my heart and keep it pure." This became a frequent prayer of mine. Anytime I found myself attracted to a boy, I would immediately stop and ask for God's intercession. By no means am I going to claim I was perfect at not daydreaming about different guys or controlling my emotions towards crushes. Yet through this simple prayer, I taught myself that when I entered such a situation, I needed to immediately turn to God and ask his opinion about the boy in question. If I couldn't bring myself to admit my thoughts and feelings to God, then maybe I should double check my intentions.

One of my favorite prayers is the meditation "Be Satisfied with Me" by St. Anthony of Padua. If you have never read it, stop right now and look it up. It was written as if God were talking directly to his beloved child. God acknowledges our natural desire for someone to love, which He gave us. The prayer makes a beautiful comment saying "Just wait, that's all. Don't be anxious, don't worry... just keep looking off and away up to Me, or you'll miss what I want to show you. And then, when you're ready, I'll surprise you with a love far more wonderful than you could ever dream." All good things come from God and this desire for love is part of how we are able to share in His goodness.

While I cannot say, I have found that perfect earthly love, Jesus has shown Himself to be my greatest suitor. I've had many occasions of asking Him to show me His love, and He provided a response faster than I ever anticipated. I recall during one specific occasion when I was revisiting the scene of a traumatic time in my life. The reality of having to go back to a place that had hurt me so greatly terrified me. God knows that one of my love-languages is receiving hugs. For the entire first week after returning to the location of the event, I was receiving multiple hugs each day. Some were from close friends, but some were people I barely knew. Ultimately, I feel that it was God sending me His love and merely using these people as His instruments.

We all have a desire to be pursued and loved while on this Earth, but I think that each person God places in our lives is to love. By loving others, we are loving God. In the same way, God is able to show us His love through those around us physically. "I want you to see in the flesh a picture of your relationship with Me... Know that I love you utterly. I AM God. Believe it and be satisfied" (Be Satisfied with Me).

Questions to Consider

1. God has a beautiful plan for your life, including who you are supposed to marry. How can we teach and help our young people learn to wait without being anxious?

2. Surrounding yourself with Christ-like friends makes all the difference in the world. Are your friends helping you grow closer to Jesus, or pulling you away?

FAITHFUL FRIENDS ARE
life-saving medicine;
THOSE WHO FEAR THE LORD
will find them.

SIRACH 6:16

~ The Gift of Godly Friends ~

Written By: Elza Spaedy

I met my husband David in Fort Lauderdale, Florida in the summer of 2000 and we got married the next spring on Saint Patrick's Day (March 17). We were blessed with our first child Bella three years later. Bree was born just 20 months after that, and then we welcomed Tristan. We felt blessed beyond belief, but we soon realized that South Florida was not the ideal place to raise our children. We also thought that it was important for our kids to grow up with their grandparents nearby if at all possible. My parents still live in Brazil, so we thought moving our young family to my husband's hometown of Bismarck, North Dakota was a good idea. We left South Florida in 2008 when the kids were 4, 2 and 6 months old. A few months after we moved, the first bitter cold Bismarck winter hit and I had a rude awakening. Years earlier I was diagnosed with fibromyalgia, which is a disease caused by overactive nerves in the body. The pain can be worse for people living in cold climates, and the winters in Bismarck were brutal. Coupled with the fact that I didn't know anyone except my in-laws, I felt very isolated. It was freezing outside, but inside I felt like a spiritual desert.

My in-laws sensed that I was feeling lonely, so they introduced us to a dynamic young couple in our new parish. We had a lot in common with Sara and Jerry Richter, and Sara and I became fast friends. We were all passionate about raising our kids in the Catholic Church. David and I were invited to a gathering they held at their house every month called simply "young adults." Every month Sara and Jerry would open their home to dozens of people seeking a closer relationship with their community, and of course with God. They would recruit amazing speakers for our gatherings that continuously put us on fire for the Faith. This special group was just what we needed, an answer to our prayers. I am so thankful to David's parents who had the wisdom to see what we needed at that time, a faith-filled support system. Some of the wives in this group would get together every week for coffee and homemade frittatas. These gatherings hold a special place in my heart because it was there that we became the Body of Christ for each other. Even though my family moved to North Carolina, I am grateful to say some of these women are still my closest friends today.

Those weekly get-togethers got me out of bed in the morning, and spending time with my new friends helped me forget about the fibromyalgia. At that time, many of us were full-time moms living in a culture that often devalues this role. We would spend hours laughing, crying, praying and watching our kids play together. I learned so much about my faith at "coffee," but what I mostly want to pass down to my precious daughters is the importance of surrounding yourself with other faithful women. It was with these new on-fire Catholic friends that I truly learned the meaning of natural family planning. In those coffee gatherings we would sometimes have 10-15 little kids running around and we all felt so blessed to be their moms. My son Tristan never went to preschool as we all felt that those weekly meetings served as their preschool. I love that our Catholic faith still stands firmly against the use of any type of contraceptive to prevent married couples from having children. Instead, our religion teaches us to be open to welcoming new life and to let God plan the size of our families.

Praise Jesus for our unchanging and consistent church teachings, and for all those married Catholic couples practicing natural family planning. What a wonderful and powerful witness in a culture that impresses upon couples that multiple children can be a burden instead of precious gifts from God. The more I learn about my Catholic faith, the more I fall in love with its teachings. Our Creator always has our best interest at heart! When so many people today are screaming for our church to change its teachings on different issues, I pray that never happens. If anything, today more than ever we need our faith to remain steadfast in its beliefs to help us navigate this crazy world we live in!

Questions to Consider

1. Think back to a time when your relationships with close girlfriends were an answer to your prayers. How did those close connections help you get through hard times? Would you be willing to start a "coffee group" to help other women battle feelings of isolation?

2. If you are done raising your children, have you thought about how you can share your wisdom with younger moms that may be feeling overwhelmed?

WE HAVE COME TO KNOW AND TO
BELIEVE IN THE *love* GOD HAS FOR US.
GOD IS *love* AND WHOEVER
remains IN *love* REMAINS
IN GOD AND GOD IN HIM.

- 1 JOHN 4:16 -

~ God's Perfect Love ~

Written by: Maggie Malcolm

Isn't it so satisfying to make your parents proud of you? As a child, I was too proud to admit being prideful myself, I thought of it more as striving for perfection. For almost as long as I can remember, I was willing to do whatever it took for this image of "perfection." Earning straight A's in school, competing on high-level soccer and basketball teams, wearing the coolest clothes- this ruled my life, even as a 4th grader. In high school there were even more awards to be won, leadership positions to fill and varsity sports to join. Don't forget the makeup, the hair, and the jewelry! Being admired by others was so important to me. Having a good reputation while also being in the "cool" group was my goal. I graduated at the top (not first, but second) of my graduating high school class, and was on my way to college on a full scholarship- half academic and half athletic. I never felt the need to brag about myself, since I thought these accolades said it all, that they defined me. My parents were so proud, and others were impressed.

I wanted so much to appear perfect, to be admired, and didn't want to taint that perception, so I hid things, and I would lie. I guess I was afraid that my parents wouldn't love me as much if they knew that I sometimes drank underage. I figured it wasn't a big deal, thinking, "I'm not as bad as that guy or that girl." But teenage brains aren't fully developed until we reach our 20's, so decisions we make then aren't always the best. Drinking underage might seem harmless when you're young, but for me, it got easier and easier to justify my bad behaviors.

Once I went to college, the party scene was everywhere. I participated while still managing my responsibilities - never skipping a class, keeping up with the extra demands of the Scholars Program, as well as learning the ropes on the lacrosse team. Going to parties with my teammates or other friends was just part of the "college experience." Yeah, I would drink so much that my memory of the night was fuzzy, but that was all part of the fun. It seemed innocent enough until it wasn't. In the early morning hours after a party somewhere, a group of us went back to a late night restaurant on campus to get something to eat before stumbling back to our dorm rooms. A recruit (prospective high school student-athlete, a girl who I was hosting for the weekend) and I stepped out of the big dining hall, probably laughing way too loudly when a police officer stopped us. "Where have you girls been?" he asked. I imagine that we both turned white as a sheet. "At a party," she said. "I'm on my lacrosse visit." He had both of us take a breathalyzer to test our blood alcohol content. I don't know what sort of numbers showed up on that test, but it wasn't good. That police officer did not like the fact that I, a student-athlete representing our university, would bring this 17-year-old high school girl to a party and get her drunk. He put me in handcuffs and shoved me in the front seat of his police car, sobbing. I spent that night in jail.

How could this happen to me?! My squeaky clean reputation, down the drain- how embarrassing! I wish I could say that after this incident I learned my lesson and left the college party scene. Unfortunately, that didn't happen. It took me years to realize how destructive something as seemingly innocent as partying in college can be. I guess I learned it in God's time. But right after being arrested for underage drinking, I did learn some valuable lessons. I dreaded having to tell my parents, which I think was rooted in a deep fear of losing their love. But through this experience of disappointing them, I learned that there is nothing I need to do to earn their love, that they love me no matter what. I realized that my relationship with God is similar. I thought that I needed to "be good" to earn His love and hide my sins to avoid disappointing Him. But no! God loves me so perfectly- I just need to let Him love me, be honest with Him, recognize my littleness and my need for Him. It's not about *me*; it's about *God's love*! Here's another lesson I learned: for someone who cares too much about what other people think and is not naturally humble, it takes a humiliating experience (like spending the night in jail) to grow in humility.

In God's time, He will continue to guide me toward Himself. He is gentle at times and harsh at others- but always loving. Enough time has passed, and I guess I have matured enough to actually be thankful for this tiny bit of suffering that God allowed in my life.

Questions to Consider

1. Describe a time in your life when you felt the pressure to appear perfect in your role as wife, mother, sister, daughter or friend?

2. How have the sufferings in your life brought you closer to God?

SHE CLOTHES HERSELF WITH
fortitude, AND FORTIFIES
HER ARMS WITH *strength.*

PROVERBS 31:17

~ The Gift of Fortitude ~

Written by: Rose Abell

Receiving a gift from someone you love is a beautiful thing, and that is especially true when the gift comes from Heaven. The Catechism states, "The moral life of Christians is sustained by the gifts of the Holy Spirit." One of the seven gifts, fortitude, "ensures firmness in difficulties and constancy in the pursuit of the good." Basically, fortitude gives us the courage to follow the will of God in any situation. This special gift helped me survive the most trying year of my life.

My husband of 46 years is divinely inspired by the Holy Spirit. Not only is he inspired, but the Holy Spirit assigns him missions surrounding the fight to end abortion. These missions from God yield great rewards, but they are not met without painful struggles sent straight from Satan.

The first mission revealed to him was to author a heart-wrenching book of poems written from the perspective of an aborted child. It all began in 2011 when we moved to North Carolina from our home state of Kentucky. Through much discernment and prayer, my son accepted a new job at a law firm in a suburb of Charlotte. My husband, son, daughter-in-law (the "daughter" I never had), and my grandson set off on this exciting adventure. We settled into our new home in Huntersville and joined Saint Mark Catholic Church. We soon realized there was something special about this church. In addition to being very welcoming, the atmosphere there is... holy. I believe now after seven years here, this is because of the Perpetual Adoration Chapel. What a beautiful experience it is to be able to walk into the chapel 24 hours a day to spend time with Our Lord. And this is where I first saw the Holy Spirit engulf my husband with his new mission for God.

In 2014, my husband and I joined a group of Saint Mark parishioners who travel to Charlotte once a week to pray outside an abortion clinic. This is something we have always wanted to do, and now because we are retired, we have the time. My first experience there was quite frightening actually. I could sense the evil surrounding the house where the killing of babies took place. I saw a big, black bird flying overhead that gave me the chills, and it was eerie to walk on the sidewalk in front of the clinic. I cried as I contemplated the horror that was taking place inside. I could feel my heart aching for all the babies who would never live, and for the mothers who would regret their decisions with agonizing heartbreak.

I found immediate comfort from the Blessed Mother while praying the rosary. My husband and I took this time to pray individually and walked separately up and down the sidewalk in front of the abortion house. After the initial shock of the environment and through the comfort of the Blessed Mother, I was shown the beauty surrounding this evil place. There was a small lake right across the street, and I noticed the early morning mist rising up from the water. Birds were chirping, and geese were squawking. The beauty of God's creation was such a stark contrast to the human evil taking place just across the street. God broke through it with the beauty of His sunshine -- bright and warm on my face. God kissed me on the cheek, and I knew His Love was there.

This is the place where my husband's spiritual mission took off. He would walk along the sidewalk praying and talking with God. That's when the Holy Spirit gave him the words to write the poems for the book "*The House Behind the Trees.*" As these poems developed, so did some critical health challenges for my husband.

Our first scare happened at the abortion mill on one of our visits during the 40 Days For Life. We were praying our rosaries, and suddenly my husband experienced a jolt of pain in his lower back. Initially, he tried to "walk it off," but the pain became too excruciating, so I rushed him to the hospital. While driving, I was praying for Mother Mary's intercession to help him. Doctors told us he had kidney stones, and the process to pass them is usually long and very painful. During this time of waiting, I continued to pray to our Mother Mary ... and She did not disappoint. From the time the pain began to us leaving the hospital after the stone passed, it was only a total of two hours! That's almost unheard of with kidney stones. The realization that this was Mother Mary's intercession is like no other conclusion that the mind makes – it is a knowing in your heart that this was an intervention by God through the Blessed Virgin – an answer to a prayer in the deepest sense. God was protecting my husband, but he would need continuing protection going forward since this wasn't the only instance of physical distress. There were other times when my husband experienced extreme pain in the kidney area, and we were forced to leave the abortion clinic. After discussing this situation with our pastor, my husband was advised that going to the Adoration Chapel in lieu of the abortion mill might provide the spiritual direction that was needed to continue his work.

Recently the Holy Spirit expanded my husband's mission to include lyrics for songs. Through this process, God has put many amazing people in our lives. At the same time, Satan is continuing his efforts to destroy my husband's missions. He has been in and out of the hospital many times in 2018 with a series of critical and disturbing medical issues. But I know through prayer and perseverance my husband will continue to pursue his purpose in life which is serving the Lord. The stress and unexpectedness of his physical pain along with fear and anxiety had become a daily routine for me. I know that as we both get older, our health can change in an instant, but when you are in the midst of major trauma, the harsh realities of our mortality become real.

The fear and anxiety of each experience became overwhelming for me. My husband's health scares were more than enough, but I found myself wondering if this was my new normal. I could no longer attend daily Mass to receive the Eucharist or participate in my regular church ministries. I was struggling with my priorities, but thanks to my parish priests and the Sacrament of Reconciliation I was given Jesus' words to help me. The schedule of daily confessions before all Masses and the fact that I was still attending Sunday Mass, gave me the strength I so desperately needed.

It was an amazing experience to talk and then listen to Jesus speak to me through His priests. It became clear to me that my priority was my vocation of marriage – taking care of my husband during these trying times. While daily Mass attendance and receiving the Eucharist are clearly important, my vocation to my husband was where I needed to be. The evil one can sometimes use the good things to confuse us and keep us from what God is calling us to do.

After one particular confession, my tears of gratitude while saying my prayers of penance were extremely cleansing; but nothing like what I experienced as I walked to my car. As I left the church and passed the fountain of flowing water, I felt a distinct and overwhelming sense of relief. It was as if someone had lifted the weight of what I was carrying off my shoulders! Jesus took my burden that day, and He continues to walk beside me.

Yes, I still experience moments of fear and anxiety but nothing like it had been. That's because I have been using the gift of fortitude. With His help, I am facing the danger and pain of my husband's mission with courage and strength. God has given us many blessings during this trial of suffering. We have realized what it really means to "offer it up" to the One who loves us so dearly and will never leave us.

Questions to Consider

1. God gives all of his children special missions in life. Has God revealed yours, and if so, how will you go about fulfilling your mission?

2. The gift of fortitude is one that helps us get through tough times without losing faith and hope. Can you describe a time in your life that this gift has helped you?

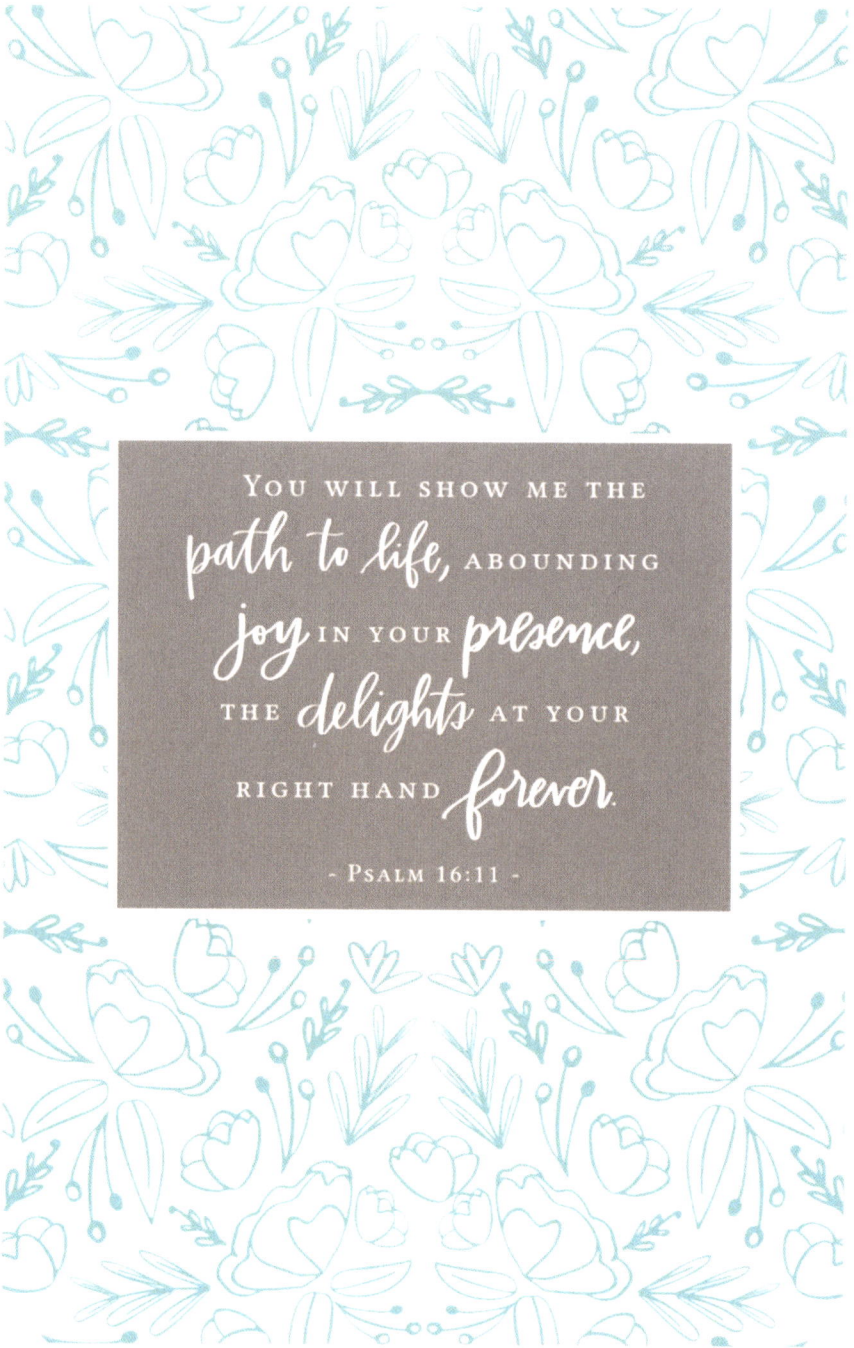

YOU WILL SHOW ME THE *path to life*, ABOUNDING *joy* IN YOUR *presence,* THE *delights* AT YOUR RIGHT HAND *forever.*

- PSALM 16:11 -

~ Fruit of Obedience ~

Written by: Veronica Brilhante

My husband Guy and I were both raised in devout Catholic families on the island of Oahu in Hawaii. Being Catholic was all we knew growing up, but in my late twenties, I began to question my faith when I started attending non-denominational bible studies. Some of the things I was learning in those studies weren't lining up with Catholic teachings. So, in my search for answers, I called the parish office of our local Catholic church. The office secretary gently and patiently answered all my questions, and then gave me some life-changing words of wisdom: "Be careful the Devil is trying to steal your faith." This was a Holy Spirit moment for me. Something stirred in my soul because I felt like these words were not from her, but from God himself! I fell to my knees and cried out to the Lord, "If you really want me to stay Catholic, you need to show me."

Shortly after that, our growing family moved to a bigger house in a different area on the island, about twenty miles away. That's when my faith journey really took off. Not only did I pray to God to show me the way to remain Catholic, but I started taking steps to become more involved with my new church. A close friend and I started a family catechism program called Family Intergenerational Religious Education or F.I.R.E. While having the privilege of teaching, I learned so much more about Catholicism and realized just how little I knew of my own religion. At the start of the new millennia, God slowly ignited the fire within me, and my love of Catholicism grew.

In August 2000, my husband sincerely approached me, saying he felt God was going to move us out of Hawaii but didn't know where. I wasn't ready to accept that, as I couldn't bear to move our children and us away from our family. The tradition in Hawaii is that you never leave "Ohana" family, and it would have been devastating to our parents to take their grandchildren away. Despite all of this, Guy started doing some research and consulted a wise and well-educated family friend asking for advice on the best place to raise a family in the mainland. He confidently and without hesitation stated, North Carolina, is one of the best places. At that time, my husband felt stagnant at his job, and we were having financial hardships while raising three sons in Hawaii. God continued to work gently and patiently on my reluctant heart over the next few years.

Our fourth child, a daughter, was born the following year, in July 2001. She came into the world just two months before the deadliest terrorist attack in history. Between having a newborn and being shaken by the devastating events of 9/11, we knew it wasn't God's timing. For the next three years, the Holy Spirit continued to place a scripture on my heart (Psalm 16:11) "You will show me the path to life, abounding joy in your presence, the delights at your right hand forever." I did not know what it meant at the time; however, meditating upon this passage helped me in the decision-making process to eventually agree to move our family to the mainland. In fact, by God-incidence, a dear friend later had this same verse framed for me as a gift. She had no clue as to how much this scripture meant to me.

Looking back, my husband Guy had always dreamed of living in North Carolina, and never really knew why. Now we know it was the Holy Spirit who put a strong desire in his heart to be here. Reflecting on our lives today, we see how God had been speaking to us through the little things at first, like finding a puzzle piece of North Carolina under the couch, and Guy coaching a boy from North Carolina.

Then, in the summer of 2004, I read an article in the Sunday paper about a local family leaving the islands and moving to North Carolina. It was a sure sign from God, I couldn't believe my eyes! We were so curious about why this family was making such a courageous move. Fortunately, we were able to meet with them, and after a long conversation, we decided to embark on this adventure ourselves. This began the most painful part of our journey: we were leaving the Ohana, and we had to figure out how to tell our parents.

Diligently we prayed, sought counsel and decided that writing a letter would be the most charitable way to reach their hearts. We were letting go and letting God. The messages, of course, were received with great shock and a lot of tears. Our parents wanted the best for us, and they knew this was God's will. This realization brought them great peace. As painful as this was for us, a joy welled up in our hearts, which we could never be able to describe in words. Without a doubt, we knew in our hearts our Lord had a plan for our lives in North Carolina.

Since my husband had been with his company for sixteen years in Hawaii, he could make a lateral transfer to Charlotte. While researching the move, we were intrigued by the welcoming family environment we read about in the surrounding cities. One suburb, Huntersville, was named one of the top cities to live in for 2004. In October, we ventured to the Queen City for a short visit to confirm our choice. We fell in love, it was everything we had dreamed it would be. The southern hospitality and the fall colors took our breath away. We attended the 5pm Sunday Mass at a local church and witnessed the reverence of the priest holding up Jesus during the consecration. At that moment, my husband and I looked at each other while holding back tears. We both knew we were home...the veil of uncertainty had been lifted as we encountered the abounding joy of His presence.

On the last day of our visit, we signed a contract for our future home in NC. In fact, we took a leap of faith and purchased the new house before my husband had an official job offer. People probably thought we were crazy to buy a home while our home in Hawaii was still on the market, but we sold our house in Central Oahu within a month of our return. In April 2005, my husband got "the call" offering him a position in Charlotte and his first words to me were "Oh ye of little faith." Fast forward to June 2005, and we were on a plane with our three sons ages fifteen, twelve, and eight, our daughter was nearly four. We left Oahu with the dream of a fresh start and traveled five thousand miles east to the Tar Heel state.

I knew our Savior didn't just bring us here to get us out of debt, it was much deeper than that. God had us on a spiritual journey to experience the fullness of our faith. Once I got settled in my new home, I joined Saint Mark Catholic Church and connected with the Women of Joy Bible study. This was a game changer for me because it was there that I finally found the "path to life." I made beautiful, godly friends who continue to give me unconditional love. However, it is the body, blood, soul, and divinity of our Lord in the Eucharist that allows me to be lifted-up. The ultimate freedom I discovered had nothing to do with leaving Ohana behind, it had everything to do with trusting God enough to follow His will.

At the beginning of Genesis 12, God told Abram to "Go forth from your land, your relatives, and from your father's house to a land that I will show you. I will make of you a great nation, and I will bless you..." It is now 13 years later, and one of our sons is married, and another is on a Catholic mission, inspiring God's word to our youth. Guy's immediate call to faith has blessed us, and God has shown us our land.

Questions to Consider

1. Have you ever been inspired to take a dramatic leap of faith? If so, how did it change you?

2. What are some of the ways we can learn to trust God more so we can clearly see His path for our life?

ALWAYS BE READY TO GIVE A

reason FOR THE *hope*

THAT YOU HAVE.

- I Peter 3:15 -

~ Self Care Is Not Selfish ~

Written by: Betsy Hoyt

True integration of mind, body, and soul can exist in life. I have come to discover my feminine heart and its place in my life as a Catholic woman. This journey of self-discovery did not come without hardships, and many lessons learned along the way.

Many years ago, in an effort to adjust to a new life as a homeschooling mom of two sons, I had taken on a low maintenance attitude toward myself. I considered it almost sinful to take care of myself because it was taking time away from my duties as wife and mother. My mindset was that my femininity wasn't nearly as essential to my sons' development as much as their father's masculinity. There were many days during those early years of homeschooling that I didn't even take a shower. I adopted what my husband called my "uniform," a velour sweatsuit. I attended Sunday Mass in a pair of slacks, a simple blouse, minimal makeup, and a chapel veil. The chapel veil meant I didn't have to do my hair.

I immersed myself in work surrounding my husband, kids, home, and parish apostolate. I did not maintain any deep friendships, just acquaintances. I thought I didn't have time for the seemingly vain activity of chatting over a cup of coffee. I used the "I'm too busy" excuse so I wouldn't have to deal with my declining wellness. This decline was manifesting itself in 40+ pounds of weight gain, a weak prayer life, lack of intimacy with my husband, daily back and neck pain, and loneliness from having no "real" friends. Truly, I was on a downward spiral, and I was in denial about it.

Suddenly, God moved His mighty hand and used our oldest son Curtis as the instrument to change the direction of my wellness. When Curtis was 11 years old, he was in a serious skateboarding accident that left him with a reconstructed jaw which was wired shut for 8 weeks. My "busy-ness" came to a screeching halt as my family's focus became the healing and comfort of our son, and helping his little brother Henry process the trauma as well. It was a daily effort to keep Curtis nourished on his liquid diet as to avoid the loss of too much weight on his already slender frame.

After one week of taking care of Curtis, the realization that I had totally "let myself go" had become clear and unavoidable. I can remember the exact moment: I was walking down the stairs after giving my son his lunch, and suddenly I felt every ounce of energy drain from my body. It was only 10 in the morning, and I had already been up and down those stairs so many times! My entire body ached, and I was completely exhausted. I thought to myself, "Betsy, you're not old, but why do you feel so old?" I turned around, went back up the stairs and into my room and cried out to God in a new way: a very personal way. I was lonely, tired, and afraid that I would never be able to feel good again. I was longing to experience true joy!

By this time I had gained 50 pounds, and I hardly recognized the woman in the mirror staring back at me. I was so overly concerned about upholding an image of the perfect Catholic homeschooling mom that I'd lost sight of the true femininity God was calling me to. Looking back on it, I can see how perfectly He used our son's accident to show me what I had become. Finally, I put my pride aside and started listening! The Lord had been reaching out to me in Adoration, but I was too busy telling Him my plans. For too long I failed to learn that His plans for me were so much better!

After the epiphany on the stairs, He set in motion significant events that would come to transform my mind, body, and soul. I started exercising and eating right. I lost all the extra weight I had gained, and I began to compete in marathons, then triathlons. This led to my certification as a personal trainer and a nutrition coach for women. I realized that if I suffered in these areas, then surely other women do too. I felt called to help others restore their health so they could also live out their vocations fully and happily.

Over the past ten years, I have had the opportunity to share the gift of intentional and integrated wellness with a broad variety of women. Integrated wellness includes prayer, exercise, and proper nutrition. Some of my clients are mothers with large families and face constant taxing challenges, others are addicted to food, and some are just trying to get a handle on their changing or aging female body. Most of these women who reach out to me do so in sheer desperation. They are looking for reassurance and a need for a more positive and realistic approach to regaining control of their wellness. All of these women long for an ear that will listen, and a companion to encourage and console them in the way only a feminine heart can. It is through our feminine genius that we can each achieve this integrated wellness each in her own way. As St. Pope John Paul II reminded us in his Apostolic Letter "Mulieris Dignitatem", the Church "desires to give thanks to the Most Holy Trinity for the 'mystery of woman' and for every woman-for all that constitutes the eternal measure of her feminine dignity, for the 'great works of God,' which throughout human history have been accomplished in and through her" (No. 31).

As women, we can easily be drawn into vanity when taking care of our bodies. Therefore, when our prayer life is active and consistent and paired with a well-ordered intentional plan of wellness, we can avoid falling into the trap of vanity.

Moderate to intense, consistent exercise continues to be a source of transformation for myself and my clients. I have witnessed first hand how consistent prayer and exercise profoundly transform the women I work with. They report how they are better equipped to move through their daily challenges, as well as to be able to express a real presence to others when needed. Their minds are calm, and their spirits are strong. A word of caution should be noted here when discussing the integration of mind, body, and soul in the realm of exercise. Many faithful Catholic women find themselves receiving physical benefits from the practice of yoga. We must be careful in this regard. Yoga is a religious practice rooted in Hinduism that Holy Mother Church warns against. As Christians, we place ourselves in spiritual danger when practicing yoga whereby we are caring for the body to the detriment of our soul.

There are alternative programs which exist. One of these is Pietra Fitness (www.pietrafitness.com). Pietra Fitness' "whole person" workouts utilize physical exercise to promote core strength as a solid physical foundation for the rest of the body. For the soul, the workouts include prayer and meditations built upon the strongest of foundations: the rock of Christ and His Church. This powerful combination truly benefits the entire human person; restoring harmony and wholeness to both body and soul.

Pietra Fitness is not "Christian yoga" nor "Catholic yoga." Most Hindu and Christian philosophers would agree that "Christian Yoga" is an oxymoron because Christianity (coming from Christ) and yoga (based in Hinduism) have fundamental differences in theology and philosophy. The practice of yoga is inherently Hindu in its spirituality; therefore, an exercise program cannot be both yoga and Christian. Pietra Fitness seeks to provide some insight into why this is true, both in general terms and through specific examples.

When we as women intentionally strive toward integrated wellness, we grow in virtue, strength, and dignity. We are women living out our vocations in mind, body, and soul turning our wellness into a living testimony of His Glory. Saint Pope John Paul II, pray for us!

Questions to Consider

1. Am I taking the time to exercise intentionally? Do I value the gift of my physical self which God has gifted me?

2. Do I honor this physical gift of self with rightly ordered self-care and prayer time?

My grace is sufficient for you, *for my power is made perfect in weakness.* Therefore, I will all the more gladly *boast of my weaknesses, that the power of Christ.* may rest upon me.

2 Corinthians 12:9

~ Finding Strength in Vulnerability ~

Written by: Christine Wisdom

I once asked a client of mine, "If you really knew that you were loved, really loved, no matter what, what would change for you?" His response was, "Everything."

The truth is, love is always available to us, but we must consent to open our hearts to receive it. "Truly I say to you, unless you are converted and become like children, you will not enter the kingdom of heaven" (Matthew 18:3). Growing up as the oldest of four children and 35 first cousins, I was raised with a great sense of responsibility to care for others and to do things, "the right way." My mother was nurturing and peaceful and deferred to my father who was authoritarian and had difficult expectations for us. I often felt that I wasn't "good enough." I struggled to feel heard and felt as though love needed to be earned. I approached my relationship with God in a similar way, feeling as though I could only come to God if I had done everything right. I felt pressure to be tough and guard my heart against disappointment. I shied away from vulnerability, especially with God. I wanted to be strong: unmoved. I stuffed my emotions which manifested in physical illness and body pain. On the outside, I was calm and seen as someone who had it together. On the inside, I struggled to feel my emotions, trust others or speak my truth without fear.

At age 15, I attended a powerful retreat at a difficult time in my life where I felt a strong calling to be a pastoral counselor. Through my studies of psychology, theology, and philosophy, I began to examine my relationship with God and learned to separate my relationship with God the Father from my relationship with my earthly father. Through the sacraments, forgiveness, and prayer, I began to understand more about the Father's love for me and became passionate about living as a part of Christ's body on earth.

When I first began my work as a pastoral counselor, I still struggled with vulnerability and was more comfortable examining thought patterns than feelings. I struggled to sit with others in the midst of their pain without trying to change it. In the last decade, the Lord has slowly been teaching me about the power of presence, being still and finding Him in the depths of suffering.

In the past few years, I have been working with trauma survivors and focusing much of my efforts on learning the developments of psychology in healing trauma. Of one thing I am now certain, that there is no true healing apart from the love of God through Jesus Christ. In the year 2018, my view of the world was turned upside down as I found myself working in challenging situations with trauma survivors, terminally ill clients and the spiritually oppressed. I was in search of healing for the clients I was working with and was preparing to speak at a healing service on Pentecost. Little did I know, I would have the opportunity to test everything I believed about the love of God and the necessity of surrender.

On Mother's Day, the week before Pentecost, I sat in Adoration, writing my talk about the Father's love for us. At one point, the inspiration stopped, and I had a sense that my speech was still unfinished. A few days later, my husband and I and our two children arrived all together for our 10-week ultrasound excited to see a glimpse of our third child for the first time. As my husband and I were watching the image of our baby, the technician was unusually quiet. Then she began asking questions. We were both sure of the time we had conceived, and the circumstances surrounding everything had confirmed for us that this was God's will. The technician was noticing that the baby was measuring small and then told us that the baby is not moving and she cannot find a heartbeat. My heart slowly began to sink, "*This can't be happening.*" Suddenly, we were filled with hope as we saw movement on the screen. Simultaneously my husband and I pointed and said, *"Right there, do you see that?! What's that?!"*

The technician explained to us that the constant movement we were seeing on the screen was not the baby's heartbeat, but just my pulse. As the reality of her words set in, my heart began to break. This sorrow is indescribable, but a part of me was still clinging to hope. My prayers, study, meditations, and work have all been centered around healing for the past weeks, months, even years. *"God, I know that you can make this baby's heartbeat, but is this your plan?"* As I walked out of the birth center that day, I had no choice but to be utterly vulnerable to God, knowing that all my hope lies in Him. In the days that followed, I began to see how our family's suffering opened the door for healing for us and for several others we came into contact with. Being in that place of vulnerability and surrender made me more available to others.

That week, as I was sharing the current news of the baby, the image of a heartbeat right next to my unmoving child came to comfort me. When I ask, *"Where are you, God in the midst of this heartbreak?"* He is showing me, *"My heart is here, broken, right beside yours."*

I began to take comfort in my knowledge that our Lord was with me during that time. As I shared my testimony and message at the Pentecost service, I felt so strongly that our Lord was there, holding me. My spirit was being lifted up by the love and prayers of others all around.

The following weeks were very difficult as my body was still holding on to the baby inside of me, and I was afraid and unsure of what to expect. I prayed that I would be able to recognize the baby's body and give honor to the soul of this child that had visited me for a short time.

It happened on a Sunday morning. I began to feel labor pains while making pancakes for my family. I felt grateful to be able to have the baby at home with my husband there and to experience the depth of grief while I held my baby's body in the palm of my hand. It's hard to describe this experience, but there in the depths of great sorrow, I had an awareness of something holy. What happens next can only be explained by the grace of God. A wonderful priest, Father Paul McNulty answered my call on a Sunday morning and brought Christ to our family. We received communion in our home, and Father Paul prayed with us and anointed me.

That week, as we were preparing to bury the baby, I was praying for a name. My 3-year-old daughter came in the next morning while I was getting ready and said to me, "Mom, I had a dream, I think the baby's name is Jimmy." Since children seem to be more sensitive to the movements of the Spirit, we decided on James, "Jimmy" for short. The day of the burial, I was breastfeeding my son and praying again for confirmation and a middle name. The name "Samuel" gently appeared in my mind, and I spoke it aloud. Samuel was not a name we had discussed, and I didn't know anyone named Samuel. When I googled it, the first meaning that appeared was "*God has heard.*" Chills went through my body as the confirmation set in. "*Okay, God.*" Even during one of the most challenging days of my life, as I was in the state of vulnerability and surrender, I felt assured that God had heard me and would not abandon me.

I felt torn at the burial and forced to surrender again as I offered my imperfect prayers while trying to manage my children and prevent them from pulling headstones off the graves. (Yikes!) Exposing my children to death so early in their lives was unexpected, but strangely, their response deepened my faith. As we were walking back to the car, my one-and-a-half-year-old son turned his head, fixed his gaze and said, "Bye, bye, Jimmy." A chill ran through my body again as I felt I was in the presence of a mystery that perhaps my children understood better than I did.

It's difficult to describe how the experiences of our lives change us. For me, everything is different now. I am living my life with new anticipation of Heaven. The anticipation of one day seeing Jimmy and all my brothers and sisters in Christ. It also changed my perspective on parenting and my own identity. When we know where we come from, it's easier to understand where we're going. When Jesus appears to Mary Magdalene after the Resurrection, he says to her, "Go instead to my brothers and tell them, I am ascending to my Father and your Father, to my God and your God." (John 20:17) In my weaknesses and experience of suffering, I am forced to come to the Father again with the vulnerability of a child. I trust that He will care for me since I am his child and so are my children. I don't fear vulnerability any longer because I realize that I am "good enough" just because I am His. I can give my heart without losing myself because my hope and my worth lies in who I am in Christ.

"Come Holy Spirit, fill the hearts of your faithful and kindle in them the fire of your love." Amen.

Questions to Consider

1. Are you living your life with the knowledge that you are loved, or is much of your time caught up in trying to earn the love and approval of others?

2. Do you see your children as a gift from the Lord? Do you recognize their identity as a child of God? How do you surrender your life and the lives of your children to the Lord each day?

REJOICE ALWAYS.

Pray without ceasing.

IN ALL CIRCUMSTANCES GIVE THANKS,

FOR THIS IS THE WILL OF GOD

FOR YOU IN CHRIST JESUS.

1 Thessalonians 5:16-18

~ Grandma Alice's Special Recipe ~

Written By: Dorothy Welsh

Alice Rosalia McCluskey (1851-1943) was my great grandmother. In many families, a recipe is handed down among generations and is attributed to a specific family member. The recipe that "Grandma Alice" left my family was how to pray. I am sure this spiritual recipe can be traced back further in our family lineage, but she is where I begin my story.

Grandma Alice was born to Irish immigrants who brought their faith with them to their new land. Arriving poor, her family worked hard, and she married another Irish immigrant who built a business, and they financially prospered. She had nine children, and my grandmother, Regina McKeever (1892-1977) was her youngest child. It is from my grandmother that I began to learn about Grandma Alice's prayer life. She told me that in her home growing up everything stopped at 3 pm. That time was called 3 o'clock prayers. All work in the house ceased, and time was spent meditating on our Lord's passion. I remember as a young girl spending time at my grandmother's house and seeing this practice continue. If you peeked into my grandmother's room at 3 pm, she was on her knees, praying. The other tradition handed down from Grandma Alice to her daughters was attending Mass frequently and praying the rosary daily.

My mother, Regina (1930-present) is an only child. She along with her parents shared a home with Grandma Alice on the south side of Pittsburgh. Grandma eventually lost her sight and could no longer work around the house. As a young child, my mother remembers her Grandmother sitting in her rocking chair praying all day. When she asked, "Who are you praying for?" The answer was "My children, their children and all the children to come." Because of my grandmother's known prayer life, my mother remembers frequent visitors to the home. After Sunday dinner, relatives and acquaintances would visit to speak privately with Grandma Alice to give her their prayer requests. Grandma had numerous clergy and religious visitors to the home to request prayers as well. She had a daughter who was a religious sister, a grandson who was a Passionist priest, and numerous nieces and nephews in religious life. My mother's impression from her was that prayer was essential and that although Grandma was an invalid, she was held in high esteem for her work of praying. I found her obituary and eight priests celebrated her funeral Mass...proof that she was a well-known prayer warrior!

I grew up in a large family in the 1960s and 70s and times were changing. My grandmother came to live with us, and I loved asking her questions about growing up in the early 1900s. Her life sounded like a romance novel to me. Looking back now as an adult, I regret asking her to repeat so many sad stories about wars, the Great Depression, illnesses and untimely deaths. Many times she would get a faraway look in her eyes, and I now realize she probably missed her loved ones very much! She was the last living member of her family. I attended Catholic schools growing up, and our family went to Mass and participated in parish activities. I knew my parents still prayed the rosary daily, and we always prayed it during car rides, but with sports and other events, my parents struggled to keep family rosaries alive. But when times were tough, or a big decision needed to be made, a rosary novena was always our family "go to" prayer. After raising their seven kids, my parents were fortunate enough to be able to attend Mass daily and make several pilgrimages to Europe.

Two years ago, we lost my father. He lived a long 92 years, and he and my mother said their rosary together every night for 66 years until the very end. Shortly after his death, my mother had a debilitating stroke. She's very frail now, and so much of her personality has changed. However, there is one constant in her life...praying the evening rosary. I was staying with her recently, and after her rosary, she was shuffling down the hall to her bedroom. I offered to assist her into bed, but she said she had more prayers to say so I helped her to her chair. I peeked in to check on her, and she was deep in prayer with her Bible and various prayer books and cards. I imagine she is praying for her children, and her children's children just like her Grandma Alice taught her and handed down as a family recipe.

In 2018, my husband Rich and I celebrated our 30th wedding anniversary. Together we are doing our best to pass down our Catholic faith to our own seven children. Now as the reality of my mother's declining health sinks in, my three sisters and I are realizing that we need to become the Grandma Alice's for our families. Her spiritual recipe will only continue through our example by demonstrating for our children the amazing power of prayer.

Questions to Consider

1. If you could only pass down one thing to the next generation what would it be, and why?

2. What can you do today to help a senior member of your community - Have you considered making the time to visit the elderly in a nursing home near you?

For I *know well* the plans I have in mind for you, says the LORD, plans for your *welfare*, not for woe! Plans to give you a future *full of hope*. When you call me, when you go to pray to me, I will *listen* to you.

JEREMIAH 29:11-12

~ God's Plans Are Always Perfect ~

Written By: Lisa Modzelewski

Many of us have seen Jeremiah 29:11 scripture verse printed on journals, cards, mugs, and even graduation plaques. It can offer hope to those who may be unsure of what the future holds or great promise for the next chapter in your life. But as I read a little further, I see not only hope in the Lord for what is yet to come, but also gratefulness in what He has already done in my life. God's plan was far more fulfilling and perfect than anything I could have thought or imagined. Allow me to explain...

It all started on December 24, 1964, when my 37-year-old mother of six began to have complications during the first trimester of pregnancy. She had just lost a baby earlier that year, and her doctor strongly advised her that if she should start spotting again to come to his office immediately and he would give her an injection to raise her hormone levels. This remedy would hopefully work to allow her body to sustain the pregnancy. So there on Christmas Eve, my mom sat with her feet up and was unable to participate in our usual family celebrations. Instead, she spent a quiet night praying and asking our Lord to bless her pregnancy. Seven months later I came into this world, and that is how my life began.

Growing up in a large Catholic home there was a constant buzz of noise and commotion of people. We were a big, lively Italian family, and my mom and dad were very much into their faith. My parents passed that faith on to their kids, and for much of my life, I believed God was calling me to do the same. I wanted to have my own large family so that I could raise my children to be strong Catholics.

As a young adult, I went to Franciscan University in Steubenville, Ohio to pursue a degree in Elementary Education. While there, I grew in my relationship with God and love for the Catholic Church. I also met a man whose passion and commitment to the Lord inspired me to an even stronger commitment to my faith. My relationship with my now husband Ed began as a deep friendship but soon developed into something even more enduring. In 1990, in the presence of family and friends we took our marriage vows at Franciscan University where we met.

When Ed and I were married, I was already working as an elementary school teacher in a third-grade classroom. It was the ideal job in my mind because it offered me the opportunity to work with kids until we had our own. God had given me a desire to nurture and care for young hearts, and I couldn't wait to stay home and raise a house full of blessings from the Lord.

When I became pregnant with our first child Paul Xavier, my decision to stop teaching was easy. After all, my vocation in life was to be a wife and mother and to raise saints to further the kingdom. My teaching job was my way of building God's Kingdom until the "real" work began. My time at home with Paul has given me priceless memories. Every morning we started the day with Mass, which included stopping at the statues of Mary and Joseph to ask for their intercession. We played in the tree fort, went to story time at the library, and waited patiently every evening for Dad to come home when the REAL fun would begin. Ed was a great father who was totally involved in raising our family.

Not long after Paul was born the Lord entrusted us again with the gift of life, and we welcomed our second son Luke Ignatius to the family. Luke fit right into the daily routine of Mass and even added excitement to the day. It wasn't always comfortable living on one income and being home with these two active boys we affectionately called "Thunder and Lightning," but I felt great joy in my calling.

When Luke was 18 months old, Ed was offered a promotion which included a move to Charlotte, North Carolina. Though it meant a departure from friends and an active faith community, we saw it as a blessing from the Lord. We moved our small family in the fall of 1999 trusting the Lord would provide, and He did! We became involved in a vibrant parish, and we believed this was an excellent time to add to our family of four. We thought this would be an easy endeavor because we had already been blessed with two healthy children. But for some reason, I couldn't get pregnant again, and after months of trying, we both became discouraged.

And so we prayed and prayed. I offered up my daily Masses, prayed novenas to St. Gerard, had my mother on her knees, went to healing services, and had the support of my friends offering sacrifices for me in hopes for the miracle of life. Yet despite my heartfelt desires for another child, I was left with the painful disappointment that God's plan was not my plan. As I look back on it, we already had two children, and now I think of so many mothers who aren't able to have even one child. We considered both domestic and international adoption, but we were competing with couples that didn't have any.

After many months of trying, my dream of a house full of children began slowly fading away. I still questioned, bargained, and begged God for more children. I struggled to fight the temptation that God did not give us more because I couldn't handle it or I wasn't good enough mom. I was embarrassed that I had the 'token two' kids that modern culture had deemed the perfect family size. My pride wanted to scream out..."We are not trying to prevent more children...we are trying to have more!"

Slowly and painstakingly I came to the realization that this may be the size of our family. This was a difficult awareness because I had no ambitions of working outside the home, and I thought that God's only plan for my life was to be a wife and mother.

With Paul in second grade, Luke in preschool and no children on the horizon, I had to take a hard look at how the Lord might be calling me to nurture young hearts. Maybe it wasn't in the way I thought. It was only when I completely surrendered my life to God's will that my heart softened, and I began to pursue my teaching license for North Carolina. I applied for a job in 2003 as a teacher at St. Mark Catholic School in Huntersville and was offered the position as a second-grade teacher. That's when a new journey began of guiding and nurturing not only my two boys but also the lives of hundreds of children.

These students are so receptive to the Gospel message and eager to know more about Jesus. Their simplicity of faith inspires me to have the same trust in our Lord. They are full of life and joy and want only to please and to be loved. This disposition pleases the Father and wants us all to have this demeanor. At daily Mass, I pray for the grace to be the teacher that Jesus was to his disciples and to have the same love for children as he did when he said: "Let the little ones come to me, do not hinder them."

In looking back at the plans God had for me, I can wholeheartedly say that He does have plans for my welfare and not for woe. And He continues to give me a future full of hope!

Questions to Consider

1.   When has God's plan surprised you?

2.   What area in our life do we need to trust God's goodness?

WALK BY *faith,*

NOT BY *sight.*

2 CORINTHIANS 5:7

~ God's Grace Is Enough~

Written By: Pat Magro

As St. Augustine stated, "In order to discover the character of people we have only to observe what they love." I will always love my father, and I would like to share how God's unending grace helped us both during his extremely challenging journey to Heaven.

I was extraordinarily blessed to have an amazing father, William. He was quiet, steadfast, obedient and loving. He was so strong, always there with a smile, and never angry. He required no accolades, no fanfare; he only existed to love his family, his country and God. He was an honorable man that willingly enlisted to fight for his country at the age of 17 in World War II. After the war, my dad married the love of his life, my mother Anne, and moved into a modest home. This home would be the place he would spend his entire life, a place he provided for all of us. Over the years this home was filled with the love of so many. My dad continued to live there even after the devastating loss of my mother from ALS. Throughout her illness, he cared for her, he fought for her, and he refused to let her give up. Eventually, she departed this world, finally free from all the pain, but her death left a gaping hole in his heart.

Years later, a decision was made to move my father out of his home and into my home because he could no longer care for himself. The home he held onto as his remaining attachment to my mother, a house he lived in for over 60 years, was locked up. He not only lost his independence but more importantly, he lost his physical connection to her.

To say routine was important to my father is an understatement. As long as I can remember, my father was a man of steady habits. Every single day he wore blue/grey clothing, black sneakers, and a cardigan sweater. He ate cornflakes and cooked the same exact meals each day of the week.

Perhaps you just imagined the famous and beloved Mr. Rogers from the children's show, well that image isn't far from the truth! Because my father resisted change in his life, the move to our home was difficult. My husband Charlie prepared our entire house and tried everything he could to help dad feel safe, secure and at home. Charlie knew just how important it was for dad to feel as independent as he could for as long as he could. My father had never been in the position of needing help from anyone. This was one of the most painful hurdles my father would have to overcome.

He was a simple man with very few needs, but as his body began to succumb to its age, his need for control increased. While he liked his routine when he was younger, he never seemed angry when things would change, that is until his body began to betray him. The truth is, I never once in all my life saw my dad mad. I know that almost seems impossible, but it's true. He would always say "it's going to be okay." He never gave up on anyone, least of all, God. But as I cared for him and he struggled, I started to see his anger and frustration for the first time. I worried that he was angry at God or worse yet, that he felt God was somehow angry with him. So many times he would say "Why doesn't God just take me already?" The changes in him were extremely painful for everyone in our family, but especially for dad. His weakness and frustration was something I would also have to overcome. For him, it was pride that he wasn't the one taking care of everything, and for me perhaps it was that he was more human than I imagined him to be.

Over the next year, he had a few falls, and few trips to the emergency room, a few stays in the hospital and a few rehabilitation stays afterward. We had physical ups and downs and emotional ones too. Throughout this time, my father was steadily increasing his prayers and daily devotion to the Holy Rosary. I wish I could say that we had long enlightening talks about Heaven; however, they were only little moments. But they were small moments of immense beauty and understanding that I could have missed if I hadn't let go of my fears and expectations of what was happening. I am so utterly thankful for these precious moments I didn't miss due to the noise in my head or his. I watched him surrender day by day, not to illness but to God's will.

Physically, things were going downhill fast, and he could no longer get up and walk on his own. He was in and out of sleep. He bore his pain with grace. At one point he slept for 24 hours, and I couldn't wake him. We thought he was going to pass and the nurses in the rehabilitation center were almost sure of it. We called everyone to come quickly, including my siblings from Philadelphia. Amazingly, he perked up when they arrived, so the search continued to find the right long term healthcare facility.

Oh, what a rollercoaster ride! Daily we couldn't tell if his body was going to give out, or if he would wake up to say he wanted to get some exercise. One day he slept almost 36 hours. On this day, I felt I needed to stay with him through the night. He was so weak that he couldn't feed himself or drink on his own, so he no longer fought me when I helped him. At one point during that night, he started to stir. Earlier in the evening, I had given him the rosary that he used every day, just hold on to. He was cold, so I covered his hands and arms but left the rosary in his hands and placed an extra blanket on him. Suddenly his hands began to move, but I decided it best just to watch him. I didn't want to disturb him. Slowly he pulled his hands out from the covers clutching the rosary. He began to raise his hands up as if lifting them up to Heaven. These were the same arms and hands that were unable to lift to eat or drink! His eyes were fixed on something or someone, and his face was so peaceful. He stayed with his arms raised high and the rosary draping from his hands for quite a few minutes. It was the most incredible sight to behold. Then, with the same ease as he raised them, he gently put them down and back under the covers.

When he woke up the next morning, he told me that he had died the night before. He said, "I hope Jesus doesn't think I reneged on him because I wouldn't do that." And he said he was disappointed because he had to come back. I asked him why he had to come back, and he said, "I don't know maybe they have a backlog up there," and together we laughed. Could this have been what St. Augustine meant by "Faith is to believe what you do not see; the reward of this faith is to see what you believe?" I knew something remarkable had happened that night, and he knew it too.

All along we were still looking for the right long term healthcare facility. At precisely the right moment, the VA called to say they had a spot for him. After everything I had witnessed with my father just a few nights before, I knew I had to leave it up to God because He was in control.

By the time I arrived, everything was in place, and my father was already resting in his new room. As I sat in the chair next to him, I couldn't help but think of all we had been through. In the past two days, all the anxiety I had felt about how and where to care for him was gone. Peace had taken its place. I began to watch him, listen to him breathe, and I noticed he was breathing very differently. The nurse told me that dad was in the transition process now, but it could take some time. She stayed with us for at least 15 to 20 minutes and slowly his breathing became more and more shallow. While she was listening to his heart, he took a final shallow breath and with a short sigh, he was no longer with us.

As much as I miss my mom and dad, I am so glad they are together with our Lord and the Blessed Mother. They were married for 70 years when our dad was reunited with his "Irish girl" in Heaven. Now I know for sure God's grace is enough to get us through the hard times. Today I feel incredibly blessed because I was a witness to God's eternal grace during my beloved father's journey home.

Questions to Consider

1. What are some of the biggest challenges adult children face when caring for aging parents?

2. Have you experienced a difficult time in your life when you relied on God's grace to see you through it?

PRAISE GOD IN HIS HOLY SANCTUARY;

GIVE PRAISE IN THE MIGHTY

DOME OF HEAVEN.

GIVE PRAISE FOR HIS MIGHTY DEEDS,

PRAISE HIM FOR HIS GREAT MAJESTY.

GIVE PRAISE WITH BLASTS

UPON THE HORN,

PRAISE HIM WITH HARP AND LYRE.

GIVE PRAISE WITH TAMBOURINES

AND DANCE, PRAISE HIM

WITH STRINGS AND PIPES.

GIVE PRAISE WITH CRASHING CYMBALS,

PRAISE HIM WITH SOUNDING CYMBALS.

Let everything that has breath give praise to the Lord! Hallelujah!

PSALM 150

~Our God Makes All Things New~

Written By: Lisa Hirsch

God abundantly blesses us in places and ways we least expect. One of my blessings and also my challenge has often been moving for my loving husband's career. In each new location, God has gifted me with beautiful friendships. Through these friendships, God has built my faith, instructed my spirit, and led me to open my heart to experience God's merciful, healing love.

Turning the clock back ten years, I was in the early months of our move from Davidson, NC to Buffalo, NY. At this point in our marriage, we had moved numerous times throughout the US and overseas with smooth transitions. Now, after this move I found myself overcome by anxiety and daily tears. After a time, my loving mother came to visit to keep me company and try to assist in resolving my anxiety.

My mother's faith is that of gold tested in fire. She is Holy Spirit filled and soaked in scriptures, just her presence brings me peace. Mom decided I needed to establish some connections with ladies in my parish, so together we signed up for a women's Bible study. To demonstrate both God's humor and ability to work through any situation, we were the only two that signed up! The instructor listened to my tearful anxiety and graciously agreed to teach the study regardless of the fact my mom was only staying for two weeks. God Bless her!

During this time, the parish was also reading Matthew Kelly's *Rediscovering Catholicism*. In a homily, the priest invited us to pray a simple prayer from the book. "Speak with God about how He is inviting you to change your life so that you can experience the freedom to be the best - version - of - yourself."

During the women's Bible study that week, we discussed this Matthew Kelly prayer as it paralleled a point in the study regarding surrendering to God's will for our lives. As hard as it may be to believe, I was terrified to pray this prayer! As seemingly simple as it reads, I was filled with such fear of what God may ask of me. I abashedly explained this to my mom and the instructor. My faith-filled mother was surprised but nonplussed. She exclaimed, "What are you afraid God might ask of you?" I replied, "I'm afraid He will ask me to become a missionary in Africa." My dear mother kindly laughed and said something like, "He's already moved you to Africa once without asking you to be a missionary, so I don't think you have to worry." Once again, showing God's goodness in giving me just the Mother I needed she said, "You can trust God. Say the prayer!"

Although my mother's conviction and encouragement melted much of my fear, I still held a resistance in my heart that was not the truth. It was not the gentle voice of the Lord, but instead, I was listening to a discouraging untruth that God's plan may not be right. My pondering question to myself: How can I trust God in our real world with a tender, fearful, and sometimes broken heart?

With the grace of my mother's prayers and God's merciful love I submitted. Standing in my bathroom, I read the prayer from the little slip of paper. I asked God how He would invite me to change my life so that I could experience the freedom to be the-best-version-of-myself.

God's beautiful answer spoke so gently to my heart, like His whisper to Elijah in the cave. It was music! What God wanted to change was to add music to my life. The beauty and ease of the message filled me with both peace and joy. As simple as this act of submission seems, it was a pivotal point in my faith life. I stood in the valley of decision in the prophet Joel's words, and God answered.

My first opportunity to add music revolved around the iPad my husband had recently purchased for me. I added beach tunes and holiday music to brighten and add joy to the winter months. Then, with the advantage of hindsight, I can now see, what I believe was the real purpose of God's call to add music to my life. Our parish was forming a women's retreat team. My role discerned by the team was to select the songs to accompany our weekly prayers and scriptures. I had no experience in choosing music, and even the thought of this made me uncomfortable. So I asked for advice from a new friend, and she taught me how to pray and select songs. Over the year my collection of worships, praise, and reflection music grew as did my experience of the Holy Spirit working so powerfully through it. Music touches memories and opens so many hearts! It allows God's merciful grace to reach deep wounds and lift burdens with healing tears. Songs of worship and praise bring God's tangible presence among us, and uplifts spirits and fills us with abounding joy and growing faith. You've heard the expression; singing is praying twice. St. Augustine said, "Singing belongs to the one who Loves." It is explained, "as we praise God in song, something of grace happens that makes it more than any other kind of song or prayer. The song of praise to God itself becomes Love as a manifestation of the love of the One who is truly Love itself."

As time passed, The Holy Spirit began to give me nudges to share particular songs with different people. I would be listening to a song, and my heart would be touched to pray for someone, or to send a link to them to ease a burden. It is sometimes still uncomfortable to trust and send someone a song with the witness statement that you believe the Holy Spirit wants to bless and uplift them. In time, God has graciously shown me the fruit of sharing songs. When people tell me about the blessings that a song brought them, my faith grows.

Through God's grace and His patient working in my life, I am experiencing more fully the tangible Presence of God. In surrendering and Letting Go and Letting God, through that simple prayer, the words of St. Augustine have reached my heart, "*You have made us for yourself, O Lord, and our heart is restless until it rests in you.*"

My mom was right, when we trust God with our hearts and our whole beings, grace and blessings abound. Let us open wide the doors of our hearts and homes with songs of praise. Hallelujah! Let everything that has breath praise the Lord!

Questions to Consider

1. What was a time in your life when praise music moved you or touched a special memory to help you hear God's voice?

2. How can we use scriptures and songs to show God's love to others?

AND I TELL YOU, *ask*, AND IT WILL
BE GIVEN TO YOU; *seek*, AND YOU
WILL FIND; *knock*, AND IT WILL
BE OPENED TO YOU.

LUKE 11: 9

~ God Takes You Seriously ~

Written By: Brenna Zeleny

A little over three years ago I found myself searching for something. I wasn't quite sure what it was. All I did know was that I didn't feel any real joy in my life. I couldn't understand why I felt this way. I have two healthy girls, a husband that loves me, good health and a beautiful home. What more could I possibly want?

The ridiculous thing is, I actually considered myself a good Catholic during this time in my life. In my mind, that meant going to church every Sunday and that was it! Sometimes I'd listen, and other times I'd daydream, but I never really understood what was going on during the Mass. I also didn't feel the need to find out anything different. Of course, I'd pray when I needed something, and I would thank God for prayers answered, but I certainly didn't feel any real connection to Him. It's so sad to say, but it's true. And if I'm being sincere, I wasn't a very nice person. I was actually kind of mean spirited at times. I would make comments about others that would then make me feel better about myself. I'd think, "Well, I'm not as bad as *that* person, so I must be doing pretty well!" I guess it felt good comparing myself to others because then I never had to look at what the real problem was – myself! If I focused on others, I didn't have to change anything about me. But deep down, I knew that something wasn't right. I just wasn't quite sure what it was, sort of like a huge hole in my heart.

Then our parish priest started talking about a program called *Alpha* and how it was a way to develop a more personal relationship with Jesus. I thought maybe this is something I should check out since I had a lot of unanswered questions about my faith. Even though I grew up Catholic and went to Catholic schools my entire life, I wasn't sure why we believed some of the things we did. I never felt comfortable asking anyone for those answers for fear of being judged or just feeling stupid for not knowing the answers myself.

When I went the first night, I was absolutely amazed at how relaxed and comfortable the atmosphere was. Everyone was so welcoming and kind, and nothing was expected of me. I didn't even have to talk if I didn't want to. As time went on, not only did I have those questions answered, I was able to talk to others and hear their points of view on different subjects, which softened my heart.

I started to have this growing need to really know Jesus. It was like a little fire was lit in my soul, and all it took was me opening the door to let Him in! I knew I wanted to change, but I just didn't know how. Jesus knew just what to do – He met me where I was, but loved me too much to leave me there. I started asking Him to transform my life, and that's when everything started to get interesting. He took baby steps with me, but slowly over time, He changed me forever!

I used to be obsessed with TV and watched a bunch of shows that weren't good for my soul. I didn't realize that once you see things, you can't erase them from your memory. A lot of what we watch on TV isn't for God; it's pretty evil stuff! Lots of sex and violence, all things that are the polar opposite of Him – but not unlike the Devil. Some of what we watch isn't that jarring; it can be more subtle. Unfortunately, the Devil is very clever, and he uses these things to persuade us to think differently. For me, it was a slow process. I began to feel disgusted and sad at what I was watching.

Then I heard a voice in my head ask me – "Why are you watching this? Do you agree with the way these people are acting/what they're saying? Are you filling your mind full of positive thoughts that lead you to God? Are you better off after watching this?" I knew the answer was a resounding NO to every single question, but it still took 3-6 months for me to let them all go. I deleted shows that I had recorded for YEARS!!! And the best part is, it felt AWESOME! I didn't miss any of them. That's what I meant about God loving me too much to leave me where I was – He knew it would take time. He is such a patient Father!

Now during this transition, I started going to daily Mass, frequenting Reconciliation more often, and praying the Rosary daily. I realized when I opened up my heart to the Holy Spirit, He truly showed me what I needed to do to get closer to Him. I also started to experience a joy that I had never had in my life. It was like I could finally see for the first time. God truly loves me and has a plan for ME!

This wasn't without some hardship – not everyone thought my change was great. My husband thought I was turning into someone he didn't recognize anymore. He wasn't sure he liked this different person. That was the scariest part - I had fallen in love with God, so now I'm going to lose my husband? But I decided to trust God and that He would take care of my marriage, and He did. I genuinely believe that our Blessed Mother helped us so much during this time. I stayed close to her and prayed for her intercession daily. Our Lord and Our Lady did not disappoint! I've seen significant changes in my husband and children, and I know that it is all due to the prayers that I've said, and many other faithful people have said that don't even know us. That's the thing – we are all part of this Body of Christ! We don't even realize that our prayers are used for all of God's children.

My life has changed dramatically over these last few years. I know it's because I finally said YES to Him. But I also understand that this is a relationship and I need to do my part by saying yes daily. This is not a one and done situation! It is something I'm going to be working on for the rest of my life. When I finally understood that He was in love with me (as He is with all of His children), it made me want to learn more about Him. God is delighted when we take the time to know Him. We were created to be in a relationship with Him. There are a lot of people in the world that are completely indifferent to Him. I should know since I was one of those people. He has plenty of graces that He would love to shower on all of us, but it's a two-way street.

A holy priest that I know and love, Fr. Mark Nolte, has said many times, "Nothing we do in this life will be more important than knowing Him, loving Him, and serving Him." God has given me a sense of joy that I never had before encountering Him. I don't feel alone anymore. I know that He dwells within me and His Holy Spirit is always around me. I have to make that conscious effort every day to surrender everything to Him. When I do this, I find that His way is better and greater than anything I could ever imagine. He wants to be a part of everything we do, all we have to do is invite Him in. He is a gentleman, He won't force His way in.

It's so wonderful to know that when I fall down or stray away from Him in any way, I can find comfort in the gift of Reconciliation. I'm so grateful for this gift so I can stay in right relationship with Him. With Him, through Him and in Him, anything is possible!

Questions to Consider

1. What is one thing you can eliminate from your life that may be keeping you from a closer relationship with God?

2. Are you ready to let God transform your life? What are some things you can do starting today that would help you know, love and serve Him better? Pick one that you can focus on this week.

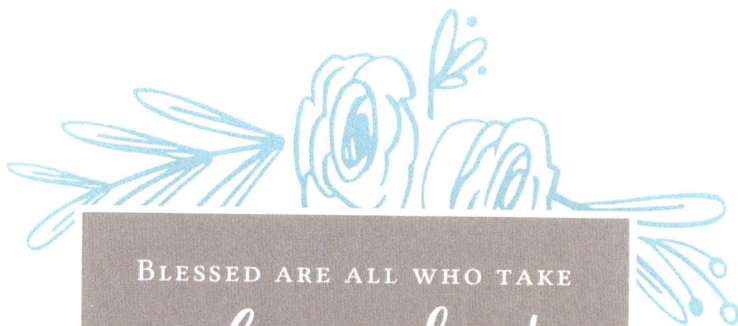

BLESSED ARE ALL WHO TAKE

refuge in him!

PSALM 2:11

~ Unfinished Business ~

Written By: Stephanie Panizza

Have you ever received a phone call in the middle of the night that your loved one is about to pass away? Have you ever had the privilege of being with someone you love in their final days here on earth? So many different emotions all at once like a rollercoaster ride that doesn't seem to end. Feelings of panic, anxiety, sadness, anger all flooding your mind at the same time. You cry out loud with pains of a tortured suffering heart. Oh God why now, not yet. I need more time. I need to let them know I love them. I forgive them. There is still so much to be said, so much to be reconciled, so many loose ends to tie up, so much more love to be given and received. Feelings of helplessness and regret. I think to myself if only I had more time I would love more, forgive more and reconcile my broken relationships. Why didn't I take care of this unfinished business? Death is final. There is no turning back. Please O God grant me this gift of a second chance. "I will praise you O Lord with my whole heart; I will tell of all Your marvelous works. I will be glad and rejoice in you. I will sing praise to Your name, O Most High." Ps 9:1-2.

The questions continue in my mind. Did I do enough in my relationship with my dad? Did I honor him the way he should have been honored? Did he see Christ in me? Is he ready to meet his Lord and Savior? Does he even know his Savior? His soul and my soul want his heart to be right before God. "God imparts himself to the soul in a loving way and draws it into the infinite depths of His divinity, but at the same time He leaves it here on earth for the sole purpose that it might suffer and die of longing for Him." (St. Faustina Diary 856) Even if he never lived his life with Christ, in the end, his soul still yearns for The Creator of all goodness.

I needed to get to him. To make sure he believed in Heaven, that he found Christ and to tell him I loved him. I wanted his path to be straight, straight to Heaven. It seemed like an eternity. I had to travel 700 miles and I was at the mercy of airplanes and schedules. I realized nothing is in my control. All I could think about was getting to his bedside. The waiting was forever. I kept thinking what can I do during this period of idle waiting? He needs the Anointing of the Sick. I could try and find a priest to administer that sacrament. But where? He didn't belong to a church. He didn't attend mass. Many phone calls were made and a priest, Monsignor Tom, agreed to go and give the anointing to my dad. He had to travel a distance, but he knew the critical situation he was in. Peace came over me. I knew then my dad would be forgiven for his sins. He was in good hands. I knew if he passed away before I got there he at least received one of the most powerful sacraments we have as Catholics. That realization that I had no control over this critical situation turned my attention to prayer, scripture, and Catholic devotionals. All I really had was hope in the Lord Jesus Christ. The faith I have been practicing over the past number of years was the foundation for my peace. The relationship I have built with my Lord Jesus Christ reminded me that He will not abandon me and He will stay close to me. He is forever faithful. "Those who know Your name will put their trust in You; For You, Lord, have not forsaken those who see you." Ps 9:10. I started my mantra of *Jesus I Trust in You.* I started reading scripture and reciting bible verses. His words brought peace. A peace that was so tranquil I could hardly understand what had taken over the panic-stricken woman I was a few hours before. I calmed down, and I knew God had renewed my strength and my will through His word. I believed whatever the outcome was going to be He would see me through it. "Those that hope in the Lord will have renewed strength. They will soar on eagles' wings, run and not grow weary, walk and not grow faint." Is 40:31.

I finally arrived at my dad's bedside. He was on life support. We didn't know if he would survive the cardiac arrest. We had to wait. The waiting was hours that turned into days. "In suffering I must be patient and quiet, knowing that everything passes in time." (St. Faustina 253). We prayed and prayed and prayed. Prayer groups were praying and fasting. The support was overwhelming. God always sends what you need when you need it. However, once again the flood of emotions took hold. Will he hear me if I tell him I love him? Will he hear this chaplet and rosary and know a little bit more about Jesus? I was still feeling regret for words unspoken and hurts that were never healed. Refocusing my attention onto God's word again, I realized that the waiting builds trust. Trust in the one who has all the control. The one who has the power to create life and to take life. "Let go and recognize that I am God." Ps 46-10. This trust that was building up inside me turned into peace. The peace that only Jesus brings. True peace arose in the waiting.

The point finally came when we would know whether my dad was going to live or die. He was taken off life support. At that moment he started to breathe on his own. It was a true miracle. A man who had no heartbeat for more than 10 minutes survived. The doctors confirmed this happens very rarely. He and I were given a second chance. I got to ask him if he heard my prayers and my words of forgiveness. He said he did. I told him Jesus Christ gave you a second chance. A chance to forgive, heal any hurts, say I love you, but most importantly to know your Lord and Savior. He accepted what I said and received Holy Communion a few days later. I found out later that week that the priest that came to anoint him blessed him, a sinner, with a relic of St. John Paul II. How AWESOME is our God!

I am forever grateful for the extra time I got to spend with my dad. But not everyone gets a second chance. Why wait until something tragic happens to get to know your Creator? Why wait to repair broken relationships? Why not forgive? "Blessed are All those who take Refuge in Him." Ps 2:11. Ask God for his mercy and grace to extend to others while there is still time. Continue to die to self. Put your pride aside and give your hurt and sorrow to Jesus so you can move forward in your relationships. "Bear all things in the name of the Lord." Say the words you want to say. I love you. I forgive you. You hurt me and this is why. Pray first then communicate. Ask Jesus for the words. See the person through Jesus' eyes not your own. Jesus said, "You shall love the Lord your God with all your heart, with all your soul and all your mind. This is the first and greatest commandment. The second is like it: "You shall love your neighbor as yourself." Matthew 22:37-39.

Love God first, live your relationships Christ-centered, and love until you die to self so that Christ shines through you to others.

Questions to Consider

1. Have you thought about what your soul would look like at the end of your life? Would it be in anguish or at peace? If in anguish, why?

2. Have you had time to reflect on the relationships that you have had over the past so many years? Are those relationships in good standing? If not, why? What can you do to reconcile those relationships?

THEREFORE, I AM *content* WITH

WEAKNESSES, INSULTS, HARDSHIPS,

PERSECUTIONS, AND CONSTRAINTS,

FOR THE SAKE OF CHRIST;

for when I am weak,
then I am strong.

2 CORINTHIANS 12:10

~ Helplessness and Humility ~

Written By: Brooke Lackey

I am an extremely independent person. I keep track of myself. I study hard. I have a perfect system. I rarely need help. I've always been this way, and recently, since entering college, I have been advised to trust more and "Let go and let God." But to be completely honest, I find it difficult to trust anyone but myself. I like to be in control of everything, and I always do it *my way*. Nevertheless, I prayed for an increase in the virtues of trust and humility.

Semester one of my freshman year went well. Although it was stressful, I enjoyed the hard work. Semester two was off to a great start. I signed up for some interesting classes, and I was mentally preparing for the insanity of my 19 credit hours. I was especially looking forward to my microbiology class because I have always been a science geek. I was preparing to study the way I usually did, with my color-coded flashcards, frequently quizzing myself, and of course, my flawless note taking. When I review, I try to avoid just memorizing things. This is a time-consuming process, and I rarely remember what I learn. My system had never failed me in the past, so I planned to stick with it.

The first day of lecture, I met my new professor. This woman stood up in front of us and essentially told us that we are to take notes exactly as she says them and memorize them word for word. If we don't, we will not do well in her class. I was livid. How dare she? I wanted to do it *my way*. My way never fails. I wanted to do it my way just to prove her wrong. But I couldn't because if I didn't do it her way, I would likely fail. I realized why I was so angry. I felt helpless. I was stuck doing something that made my life 10 times harder, and there wasn't a single, solitary thing I could do about it. I was helpless, and I hated it.

A week later, I was still angry and griping about the audacity of my professor when the New York verdict was announced. Abortion was now legal in the state of New York up until birth. I was so angry, sorrowful, and confused. The March for Life in Washington was just 5 days earlier. Did we fail? How could we let this happen? I was heartbroken. I wanted to do something, but what could I do? Once again, I felt helpless. I was powerless against some force that I had no control over. I went to Confession that night, and told the priest about the professor I despised, and asked for his advice. How was I supposed to survive this semester? I told him I wanted to fight back, prove her wrong, and to prove myself right. He said I could do one of two things: I could fight back and be miserable for the duration of the class, or humble myself, submit to her rules, and maybe learn something.

The next night I went to sit with our Lord in Adoration. I was prayer-venting about my microbiology professor when the Holy Spirit made something clear to me. Humility, helplessness, and trust all go together. No one is proud of how helpless they are, and who needs to trust in God if you think you can do it all on your own? I have been praying for a while for an increase in trust, yet I refused to surrender to God because I thought I could do it all on my own, *my way*. I was playing the game of St. Augustine: "I'll trust you, but not on this. Or that. Or that other thing. But please, give me the grace to trust."

I was close to tears in Adoration, so overwhelmed by all the work I had to do and how little time I had to do it. Finally, everything made sense. I realized I am powerless, and doing things my way isn't going to work. I have to humble myself and trust that God will take care of it. His way is always better than my way. St. Paul tells us to boast of our weaknesses for when we are weak, then we are strong. A little helplessness will show you that you are not strong enough, and trust in God shows you that you don't have to be.

Questions to Consider

1. What are the ways in which you fail to trust in God, and instead rely on your own power, work, or effort?

2. How can we practice humility in our everyday lives?

Honor your father and your mother, AS THE LORD YOUR GOD COMMENDED YOU, THAT YOUR DAYS MAY BE LONG, AND THAT IT MAY *go well with you* IN THE LAND THAT THE LORD YOUR GOD IS GIVING YOU.

DEUTERONOMY 5:16

~ Family Traits That Bind Us ~

Written By: Elza Spaedy

The summer of 2018 is one that I will forever hold dear in my heart for a few different reasons. One of them being the fact that I took a month trip to Brazil to visit my parents and got to bring my two precious daughters Bella (15) and Bree (13). Planning that trip with my girls was so much fun and getting to spend all the special quality time with them is something that I am very thankful for and hope to do more of in the future.

When you travel those long distances and have to take multiple flights (in our case it was four) it can be challenging. We arrived in Recife after our 9-hour flight from Ft. Lauderdale to find that we had missed our connecting flight to Sao Paulo due to our international flight being delayed about 2 hours. There were so many of us on that international flight that had missed our connections, and Azul airline was doing their best to accommodate all of us and make sure that we all got to our final destinations as quickly as possible. But that caused a challenge, and many of us had to be taken to a hotel (all expenses paid by Azul) to spend the night and wait for the next available flight the next day.

We were one of those people that had to be sent to a hotel... My girls were such troopers. They never complained and looked at the whole inconvenience as an adventure. Unbeknownst to us, the airline sent us to a beachfront hotel for the night. As we were approaching the hotel being driven by a cab, my girls looked at me and said: mom isn't that the ocean? And I responded yes it sure is...and they both happily exclaimed: I wonder if we are staying around here? Not long after they said that the taxi driver pulled into this lovely hotel right on the ocean drive.

That night after having a delicious dinner at the hotel the girls and I spent some time with other stranded passengers on the hotel's rooftop admiring the beauty of the ocean across from us. What a great lesson for all of us there - sometimes the unexpected can turn out to be one of the highlights of your trip.

We finally got to my parents after two days of traveling and soon forgot all the inconveniences of hours spent waiting on delayed flights and the lack of good sleep. Being surrounded by all the love from my parents and family helped Bella and Bree understand why in the big picture what we had to go through to get there was inconsequential. It did not take us long to get used to the slower pace of Brazilian life. The girls got to spend a lot of time with their cousins and reconnect with them after not seeing each other for a few years. What I had the pleasure to observe is that for kids it's so easy to pick up where they left off, and it was like they all lived down the street from each other.

I think both girls said it more than once how much they loved having my undivided attention. And I have to admit that as much as I missed my husband and my son Tristan, I loved being able to give all of me to my girls and my parents. I will never forget all the uninterrupted talks and the lazy afternoon naps we took on the hammock. The simplest of pleasures!

Another reason why this trip will be forever etched in my mind is the fact that while the girls got to spend time with their cousins, I got to spend much needed time with my mom and dad. Watching my mom patiently take care of my 91-year-old dad who for the last few years have come down with some type of dementia was a life lesson I will never forget. If you have ever dealt with someone you love having this disease you understand the pain that comes from it. Seeing my dad going from being someone who was always independent and very much the picture of good health including going horseback riding regularly into his late 80's has been difficult on the whole family. Everything started when he could no longer find his way home, and my brothers would sometimes see him sitting on a park bench telling them that he just didn't remember how to get back. That escalated into the fits of rage that's also associated with this terrible disease. I have to be honest and say that my siblings that live in Brazil have had to deal with the worst of it and I'm thankful for them being there for mom and dad. I have often felt the guilt that comes from living so far away and feeling like there's not much I can do for them. So many times I have wished I lived down the street from them so I could go over and release my mom and just sit quietly with my dad while she goes and gets her groceries or gets her hair done. I know that pain is even more significant for her, because she's the one that suffers the most seeing the man she has loved for 60 years deteriorate and have to be treated like a child again. I remember when it became clear to all of us that dad could no longer drive and my siblings had to intervene and take away the car key. As you can imagine that did not go well with him, but thankfully by the grace of God, he finally let go of wanting to drive.

All his life my dad never liked taking medicines and he never really had to since he was always very physically fit and healthy- this has caused a big challenge now that he absolutely needs to be on a few different ones. My mom has learned to be smart and hide his medicine in his food or drink by the doctor's orders. It doesn't always work, but she's doing her best. Without his medicine, my dad wanders the streets and has been found trying to cross the road without waiting for the walking sign to come on. My mom has shared that in one very scary occasion he almost got hit by a car if not for an onlooker that pulled dad away from the incoming traffic. How sad this disease is! After those close calls, he doesn't even try to go out by himself anymore. Thank God for that!

Having all that time to spend with my parents helped me ponder on what I felt was the worst part of this disease and what it has robbed from my dad and from all of us. For me it came down to this- Dad, who was always such a great storyteller, could no longer hold a meaningful conversation with anyone. That realization was a very painful one because I loved sitting with him to listen to his stories. Growing up my friends would tell me how they enjoyed coming over to my house so they could listen to all of dad's stories. And he had lots of them! He could recount things that happened fifty years ago like it was yesterday. It broke my heart that on the day the girls and I were leaving to come home, my dad exclaimed: "Where are you going, honey?" "We are going back home to David and Tristan dad..." I responded. And he said: "But you just got here yesterday!" We had been there all that time, and he thought we had just gotten there.

One of my favorite stories he used to tell me was the one about his grandmother, my great grandmother that I never got to meet. He would tell me how I was so much like her. And knowing how my dad was very fond of his grandmother made me want to ask questions about her. He would proclaim very proudly that she was a woman of great strength, with a feisty personality and very much a doer. And he would always finish with: *You are just like her.* I remember feeling very happy being compared to someone that I knew my dad loved so much. He was not a very touchy/feeling, hugging type of dad but when he told me those stories, I could feel his love for me. Maybe that's why it was so hard for me to realize that he can no longer tell me those stories. That was my dad's love language with me, and it was all gone now. I hate this terrible disease and what it has done to my dad's mind!

I had to add this story to the book once God helped me see that my love for storytelling was passed down to me from my dad and it wouldn't be right If I didn't give him the credit he deserves. Looking back now I see how the inspiration for this book, which came to me in October, is very much connected to my unforgettable summer trip spent with my family in Brazil. Through watching my dad lose the ability to do something that he had had a special gift for I have realized that maybe the storytelling doesn't have to end. It just needs to get started again by the next generation. I know that I'm not worthy of taking dad's place of storytelling, but I pray that with God's help I can be half as good as He was. And maybe, just maybe, I can inspire others to do the same.

Questions to Consider

1. Good or bad, we all inherit traits from our parents. As I grow in my faith, I realize that I used to focus way too much on the negative part of that. Thankfully God has helped me learn to look at all the wonderful things both of my parents have taught me. Do you think it may be time for you to consider the same?

2. Can you think of one thing that your parents have passed down to you that has made you a better person? Take the time to thank them today if you can.

Meet the Collaborators

	Jennifer Creter *He Comes First* Committed Catholic, Tom's wife, Aidan & Will's mom, writer, editor		**Jean Whelan** *Two Marys Guide Me From Heaven* Founder of Women of Joy, mother of 4, married to Jerry for 32 years
	Erin Zamora *My Path to Surrender* Wife to Daniel, Stay-at-home mom to 4 children		**Ann Winkle** *Worth Waiting For* Founder of Mary's Way, Catholic speaker, Life Coach specializing in ADHD
	Alexandra Stanley *Trusting His Plan* Senior at the University of North Carolina at Chapel Hill		**Kristyn Keenan** *When I'm Afraid, I Will Trust in Him* Married to Brian, mother to Grace, Alasdair, and Rosalind, photographer, and government contractor

	**Caitlin Bristow** *Using Your God-given Gifts* Wife and mom of 2, owner and hand-letterer behind *Lettered Life*.
	**Mary Meixner** (Jennifer Creter's Mom) *Christ Is Counting on You* Jim's wife for 56 years, mother of 5, grandmother of 14, great-grandmother of 3, graduate of the Lay Pastoral Ministry Program
	**Kristin Winkle Beck** *Learning to Rest in Him* CEO of Pivot Point Professionals, Executive and Career Coach
	**Sarah Miller** *Finding Peace and Joy in Doing God's Will* Wife to Larry, mother to Jacob and Katie, and Servant of God
	**Olivia Shingledecker** *Authentic Femininity* High school senior and founder of Catholic Girl Talk
	**Katie Miller** *Allowing God to Pursue My Heart* Student at Belmont Abbey College

Maggie Malcolm *God's Perfect Love* Devoted wife and mother of 2 young boys, occupational therapist, facilitator of Mothering with Grace	**Rose Abell** *The Gift of Fortitude* God's beloved daughter,wife of Doug of 46 years, mother,mother-in-law grandma
Veronica Brilhante *Fruit of Obedience* Mother of 4, married to Guy for 31 years, gardener and wedding coordinator	**Betsy Hoyt** *Self Care Is Not Selfish* Pietra Fitness Foundations certified instructor, Creator of the "Integrated Catholic Woman" wellness retreat
Christine Wisdom *Finding Strength in Vulnerability* Pastoral counselor and psychotherapist, Owner of Wisdom Integrative Counseling, PLLC	**Dorothy Welsh** *Grandma Alice's Special Recipe* Independent Cabi Stylist, married for 30 years to Richard, and mother of 7

Lisa Modzelewski *God's Plans Are Always Perfect* 2nd grade teacher at St. Mark School, Missions Coordinator at Saint Mark Church	**Pat Magro** *God's Grace Is Enough* One of The King's kids, Charlie's wife for 54 years, mother of 6, grandmother of 26, and great-grandmother of 18
Lisa Hirsch *Our God Makes All Things New* Wife of Patrick for 29 years, Intercessor / Healing Ministry, aunt of 13	**Brenna Zeleny** *God Takes You Seriously* Wife of Chris, mother to Elizabeth and Abigail, elementary school teacher, sings in her church choir
Stephanie Panizza *Unfinished Business* Disciple of Jesus Christ from Davidson, NC, mother of two	**Brooke Lackey** *Helplessness and Humility* Nursing major at The Catholic University of America. Enjoys embroidery and playing viola

Acknowledgements

A special thanks to my dear friend Jennifer Creter who was a godsend by helping to edit the book and was my right hand on this project. I will be forever grateful to you Jen.

To my sweet friend Caitlin Bristow who used her artistic gifts to come up with the beautiful cover and the artwork throughout the book. You are amazingly gifted, Caitlin. And Thank you for helping me with the very daunting self-publishing process. I truly don't know how I could have finished the book without yours and Bella's help. I'm looking forward to working with you again on my next projects.

To all the women who said yes to sharing their stories. Your courage has inspired and humbled me. Your love and faithfulness to this project have once again reminded me of how very blessed I am to have so many faith-filled friends. Without your stories, this book would not exist. This is your book! Please know that you are in my prayers daily.

To Father John Putnam and Father Paul McNulty for encouraging and supporting this project from the very beginning. Your leadership has been instrumental in making sure our personal stories align with Church teachings.

To my daughter Bella who was Caitlin's assistant during the creative and the self-publishing process. And thank you for insisting that we add all the collaborators' pictures at the end of the book. I'm glad I listened to you, honey!

To Christine Wisdom for writing the foreword. You are an amazing woman, and I'm blessed to know you. To my friend Kristyn Keenan for sharing her gift of photography by taking the beautiful pictures of the collaborators and our family picture. To my friend Sue Pompili who's an English teacher and helped with the final editing.

Finally, I would like to thank God for sending the Holy Spirit to inspire me, and for putting all the right people on my path to help me accomplish this task. We truly serve an amazing God!

About the Author

Elza grew up in Brazil with her mother and father and ten brothers and sisters. Her parents, Maria and Samuel, have been married for 60 years. Elza's mother continues to be a significant influence in her life as an example of how to be a devoted wife and loving mother. Elza lives in Huntersville, North Carolina with her husband David of 18 years and their three children Bella, Bree and Tristan where she works as a Realtor. She is the founder of a women's apostolate and the *Mother-Daughter Spiritual Brunch*. She loves God above all things and has a special connection with the elderly which she regularly visits at the nursing home near her church. Elza loves to entertain and enjoys preparing and sharing a great meal with her family and friends. One day she would like to take a trip to the Holy Land to walk in Jesus's footsteps. But for now, she's happy sharing the love of God with others around her.

62995562R00093

Made in the USA
Columbia, SC
07 July 2019